For Capital Punishment

To the memory of my friends
Martin Diamond and Herbert J. Storing

CONTENTS

Contents

ACKNOWLEDGMENTS

THIS BOOK was begun during a year's leave of absence from my regular teaching assignments made possible by a grant from the U.S. National Institute of Law Enforcement and Criminal Justice, whose Director at that time, Gerald M. Caplan, first encouraged me to undertake the task. I am grateful to the institute and to the various members of its staff who have assisted me at various points. The book was completed with the assistance of a grant from the Earhart Foundation, and it is a pleasure once again to express my gratitude to the foundation and its President, Richard A. Ware, for their support over the years. I was fortunate to count among my friends at the University of Toronto Professor J. Ll. J. Edwards who, as Director of the university's Centre of Criminology, invited me to join the centre as a Visiting Fellow during the year of my leave; this provided me not only with an office and convenient access to the Criminology Library, but with the opportunity to learn from Professor Edwards and his associates. He and they were unfailingly generous with their time, and although I learned less than they had to teach, that, as is frequently the case, was the fault of the student, not of the teachers. Charlotte Mudge and Catherine Matthews, Librarians of the Centre of Criminology, and their associates, Dorothy Chunn and Pearl Hsing, taught me to use the collection and found the materials I needed. I could not have done this work without their assistance. Nor could I have written the section of the third chapter dealing with the deterrence question without the instruction in regression analysis provided by my friends N. K. Choudhry and Abram Shulsky.

Acknowledgments

My debt to Professor Werner J. Dannhauser of Cornell University, formerly my colleague and always my friend, is a special one. He read the entire manuscript, and he and I know how much better it is because of that. Only he knows how much better it could have been.

For Capital Punishment

Introduction

IT MUST BE one of the oldest jokes in circulation. In the dark of a wild night a ship strikes a rock and sinks, but one of its sailors clings desperately to a piece of wreckage and is eventually cast up exhausted on an unknown and deserted beach. In the morning he struggles to his feet and, rubbing his salt-encrusted eyes, looks around to learn where he is. The only human thing he sees is a gallows. "Thank God," he exclaims, "civilization." There cannot be many of us who have not heard this story or, when we first heard it, laughed at it. The sailor's reaction was, we think, absurd. Yet, however old the story, the fact is that the gallows has not been abolished in the United States even yet, and we count ourselves among the civilized peoples of the world. Moreover, the attempt to have it abolished by the U.S. Supreme Court may only have succeeded in strengthening its structure.

I do not know whether the intellectual world was surprised when, only two days before the nation's two hundredth birthday, the Supreme Court held that capital punishment is not, under all circumstances, a violation of the Eighth and Fourteenth Amendments. I do know, or at least have very good reason to believe, that the Court's decision came as a bitter blow, not only to the hundreds of persons on death row who now faced the very real prospect of being executed, but to the equally large number of persons who had devoted their time, talent, and, in some cases, their professional careers to the cause of abolishing this penalty.

They had been making progress toward this end. Only four years earlier, the Court had held that the manner in which death

3

sentences were being imposed by judges and juries—discriminatorily or capriciously—constituted cruel and unusual punishment, and this decision seemed to be an inevitable step along the path described by still earlier decisions, a path that would lead ultimately, and sooner rather than later, to the goal of complete and final abolition. True, there were four dissenters in the 1972 cases, and Justice William O. Douglas, one of the five justices in the majority, had since retired; but the abolitionists had reason to hope that some of the 1972 dissenters would reconsider their positions. Chief Justice Warren E. Burger, for example, had indicated his sympathy for the abolition cause, saying that if he were a legislator making a political judgment rather than a judge making a constitutional judgment, he would either vote to abolish the penalty altogether or restrict its use "to a small category of the most heinous crimes."[1] And in a poignant opinion, Justice Harry A. Blackmun had spoken of the "excruciating agony" of having to vote to uphold death sentences, and of the depth of his abhorrence of the penalty, "with all its aspects of physical distress and fear and of moral judgment exercised by finite minds."[2] Perhaps he could be prevailed upon to set aside his constitutional scruples; after all, one year later he wrote the Court's opinion invalidating the abortion laws,[3] and that opinion was at least as bold in its disregard of constitutional scruples as anything the abolitionists were asking of him.

Besides, judges are not immune to popular opinion or able to isolate themselves completely from the trend of the times, and the trend was clearly in the direction of abolition. Juries seemed increasingly unwilling to impose the sentence of death, in other countries as well as in America. Whatever the case in the Soviet Union and Saudi Arabia, civilized countries were abolishing the penalty, whether in practice, as in France, or by statute, as in Britain. Less than two weeks after the Supreme Court held it to be not unconstitutional, the Canadian House of Commons voted to abolish it for all crimes, thus bringing to a successful conclusion a campaign that had engaged the passions of many of that country's most dedicated intellectuals. Rather than to doubt the outcome, abolitionists had cause to wonder why it had taken—and in America was taking—so long. It must have seemed to them that every decent and thoughtful person supported their cause—Albert Camus, for example, and Arthur Koestler—and the public had long since demonstrated its opposition to punishments considered by them to be less barbarous than the death penalty. This generation of Americans, unlike their forebears, would not, it is said, support the branding of convicted criminals or "ear-cropping." Public opinion was, as the Court had said as early as 1915, becoming more enlightened on these matters, and the cause of this enlightenment was a growing appreciation of "a humane justice."[4] This growing enlightenment had constitutional significance because the meaning of "cruel and unusual" varies with the times. As the Warren Court said in 1958, this Eighth Amendment term derives "its meaning from the evolving standards of decency that mark the progress of a maturing society."[5] There was, therefore, good reason to believe, and certainly good reason to hope, that by 1976 society would have matured still further and that the Court would acknowledge this officially by declaring the death penalty to be "cruel and unusual" according to the standards then governing. It was this hope that was cruelly dashed by the decision in *Gregg* v. *Georgia*, the leading 1976 case.[6]

Perhaps the Court began to doubt its premise that a "maturing society" is an ever more gentle society; the evidence on this is surely not reassuring. The steady moderating of the criminal law has not been accompanied by a parallel moderating of the ways of criminals or by a steadily evolving decency in the conditions under which men around the world must live their lives. In the short period during which the first draft of this book was written, two attempts were made on the life of the U.S. president; a former president of the Teamsters Union was

5

abducted and probably murdered; a famous heiress was indicted, then convicted for her part in an armed bank robbery; two Turkish ambassadors were gunned down; a daughter of a former president, himself the victim of an assassin, narrowly escaped death from a bomb exploded in a London street; a Puerto Rican separatist group claimed credit for simultaneous bombings in New York, Washington, and Chicago; a Dutch businessman was held captive by Irish Republican Army gunmen who threatened to chop off his head if the police made any attempt to rescue him; three or four other IRA gunmen held an innocent husband and wife hostage in their London flat, while their associates tossed bombs into London restaurants; Portuguese mobs sacked the Spanish embassy; two American diplomats were kidnapped; Lebanese private armies fought a civil war in the streets of the formerly peaceful Beirut; the American ambassador to the country was murdered; the usual handful of political murders were committed in Argentina, and the usual number of Palestine Liberation Organization bombs went off in Jerusalem; eleven persons lost their lives when a terrorist bomb exploded in La Guardia airport; South Moluccan terrorists took possession of a Dutch train and of the Indonesian embassy, shooting some of the many innocent hostages they held; and, to skip over a few months and more than a few similar outrages, the newly appointed British Ambassador to Ireland was blown up, and Palestinian terrorists seized an Air France plane and held its hundreds of passengers hostage at Entebbe airport. A person could be excused for thinking not only that the world was becoming a more savage place, but that the Israeli raid on that airport and rescue of those hostages was almost the only happy event to make the news during this period. For once a liberal democracy was seen to possess the moral strength required to defend itself. That has not often happened lately, which is why it was so exhilarating.

And it is moral strength, or the strength that derives from the conviction that one's cause is just, that is required not only to mount operations against foreign terrorists but to respond in an appropriate manner (which may mean severely) to domestic criminals. Those who lack it will capitulate—in the one case by paying the ransom demanded and in the other by refusing to impose the punishments prescribed by the laws—but will conceal the fact of that capitulation behind a cloak of pious sentiments. I witnessed this phenomenon at first hand in 1969 when armed students forced Cornell University to set aside punishments duly and fairly imposed on a handful of students who had deliberately broken its laws and flouted its authority. To justify its capitulation, the administration pointed to the guns the students had pointed at it; to justify its acceptance of the administration's capitulation, the faculty, the next day, pointed to student opinion and the presumed necessity to act only in accord with it. But the popularity of the capitulation could not conceal the fact that Cornell had proved to be an institution incapable of defending itself because, as it turned out, it had nothing to defend. An institution that lacks strength of purpose will readily be what its most committed constituents want it to be. Those who maintain our criminal justice institutions do not speak of deferring to public opinion but of the need to "rehabilitate criminals"—another pious sentiment. The effect, however, is the same. They impose punishments only as a last resort and with the greatest reluctance, as if they were embarrassed or ashamed, and they avoid executing even our Charles Mansons. It would appear that Albert Camus was right when he said that "our civilization has lost the only values that, in a certain way, can justify [the death] penalty."[7] It is beyond doubt that our intellectuals are of this opinion. The idea that the presence of a gallows could indicate the presence of a civilized people is, as I indicated at the outset, a joke. I certainly thought so the first time I heard the story; it was only a few years ago that I began to suspect that that sailor may have been right. What led me to change my mind was the phenomenon of Simon Wiesenthal.

Like most Americans, my business did not require me to

think about criminals or, more precisely, the punishment of criminals. In a vague way, I was aware that there was some disagreement concerning the purpose of punishment—deterrence, rehabilitation, or retribution—but I had no reason then to decide which was right or to what extent they may all have been right. I did know that retribution was held in ill repute among criminologists. Then I began to reflect on the work of Simon Wiesenthal, who, from a tiny, one-man office in Vienna, has devoted himself since 1945 exclusively to the task of hunting down the Nazis who survived the war and escaped into the world. Why did he hunt them, and what did he hope to accomplish by finding them? And why did I respect him for devoting his life to this singular task? He says that his conscience forces him "to bring the guilty ones to trial."[8] And if they are convicted, then what? Punish them, of course. But why? To rehabilitate them? The very idea is absurd. To incapacitate them? But they represent no present danger. To deter others from doing what they did? That is a hope too extravagant to be indulged. The answer—to me and, I suspect, everyone else who agrees that they should be punished—was clear: *to pay them back*. And how do you pay back SS Obersturmführer Franz Stangl, SS Untersturmführer Wilhelm Rosenbaum, SS Obersturmbannführer Adolf Eichmann, or someday—who knows?—Reichsleiter Martin Bormann? As the world knows, Eichmann was executed, and I suspect that most of the decent, *civilized* world agrees that this was the only way he could be paid back.

This, then, is a book in support of capital punishment. It could be entitled "the morality of capital punishment" because, as I see it, the argument about it does not turn on the answer to the utilitarian question of whether the death penalty is a deterrent; as I show in the third chapter, the evidence on this is unclear and, besides, as it is usually understood, deterrence is irrelevant. The real issue is whether justice permits or even requires the death penalty. I am aware that it is a terrible pun-

8

ishment, but there are terrible crimes and terrible criminals: Richard Speck, killer of eight Chicago nursing students; Charles Manson and his "family," killers of actress Sharon Tate and others; and Elmer Wayne Henley and the man for whom he "worked" (and whom he eventually murdered), Dean Allen Corll, the leader of the Houston, Texas, homosexual torture ring, killers of some twenty-seven young men. Henley was sentenced to 594 years in prison, but it is questionable whether even that sentence is appropriate repayment for what he did. I am also aware that "retribution has been condemned by scholars for centuries," as Justice Thurgood Marshall remarked in the 1972 death penalty cases, and that he also said, and said with some authority, that "punishment for the sake of retribution is not permissible under the Eighth Amendment";[9] but I am not persuaded (nor, as it turned out in 1976, was a majority of the Supreme Court).

I am, finally, aware that genuinely honorable men have argued powerfully and passionately against capital punishment—the first chapter of this book presents a review of their arguments, and I have made every effort to present them honestly —but, obviously, I disagree with them. I disagree most of all with the misguided, and occasionally even absurd, sentimentality that characterizes their position. Consider the reaction of the American Civil Liberties Union to the scheduled execution of Gary Gilmore, the first person (and, as I write, the only person) to be executed in America since the Court's 1976 decisions. The ACLU had recently insisted that Karen Quinlan had a "right to die," although, of course, there was no way to ascertain whether *she* wanted to exercise that right, and that a court of law had the authority to order the removal of the various life-support devices that (it was then thought) were alone keeping her alive. Now, with equal passion, it insisted that Gilmore, a convicted murderer who wanted to be executed, did not have a "right to die" and that no court had the authority to order his death.

I must also point out that I learned soon enough that it was impossible to discuss capital punishment without discussing punishment in general; our penal system, so inadequate and increasingly seen to be so, is in large part the result of our attempt to avoid punishing criminals and, above all, to avoid executing them.

CHAPTER I

The Case Against Capital Punishment

THE BIBLICAL ARGUMENT

THE FIRST MAN AND WOMAN violated God's commandment and were banished from paradise. Their first-born son killed his brother, and God made him a fugitive and a wanderer upon the earth, forbidding the soil to yield up its fruits to him, and put a mark on him, "lest any finding him should kill him." Vengeance, said the Lord, is mine, and if anyone kills Cain, it shall be taken on him sevenfold. "And Cain went out from the presence of the Lord and dwelt in the land of Nod, on the east of Eden."[1] Both homicide and its punishment are almost as old as history, and the disagreement over who shall impose the punishment, and what that punishment should be—death or banishment—followed immediately upon the first homicide.

Then Adam's wife bore him another son, Seth, to replace Abel slain by Cain, and the generations of Seth multiplied on

11

the face of the earth. With them, however, went wickedness, making the earth corrupt in God's sight, until he resolved to destroy it, putting an end to all flesh. But Noah was a righteous man, "perfect in his generations,"[2] and God spared him and his family, and gave him dominion over every living creature, and made a covenant with him, promising never again to destroy the earth with a flood but, in exchange, requiring a reckoning of him. "At the hand of every man's brother will I require the life of man," and "whoso sheddeth man's blood, by man shall his blood be shed; for in the image of God made he man."[3] It would seem, then, that in the eyes of God murder is one of the worst of offenses because to kill a man is to kill a being fashioned after God.

From the three sons of Noah the nations spread abroad on the earth after the flood, and, in time, to his favored nation God gave the law, and with it, again, the specific prohibition of murder: "Thou shalt not kill."[4] God gave men the law, but, in fashioning them in his own image, he also made them aware of themselves and of their interests, and endowed them with reason, whereby they might know good and evil, and with passions—anger, for example, and envy—and thereby made it both possible and likely that they would break the law. Perhaps it would be more accurate to say that he endowed them with these qualities and therefore found it necessary to give them the law to guide and restrain them. But men have never ceased to kill their own kind. They have killed in war, they have killed in anger or out of envy for gain, and they have enacted their own laws authorizing them to kill those who violate the laws of God or what they understand to be the laws of God. In doing these things—even, it is insisted, the last of them—they have violated God's law which forbids all killing of men, even that done under the authority of law. This is the first argument against capital punishment; it is first because if it is accepted there need be none other.

Of course, the biblical texts leave some doubt as to this, to say the least. The question is whether in giving the law to Moses and the Jewish nation, God also gave them the authority to punish infractions of the law. God commands us not to kill, but the context suggests that this commandment, like the others forbidding theft and adultery, for example, and false testimony, is addressed to the individual person rather than to the legal community. God was addressing the legal community, or would appear to have been doing so, when he said, "And he that killeth any man shall surely be put to death,"[5] and most emphatically when he said, "ye shall take no satisfaction [or ransom] for the life of a murderer, which is guilty of death: but he shall be surely put to death."[6] Even so, there have been those who argue that these passages are susceptible to other interpretations; the Genesis passage ("whoso sheddeth man's blood, by man shall his blood be shed") has been said to be a prediction, rather than an authorization to the legal community to impose the penalty of death on murderers, a prediction that acknowledges that men will frequently shed the blood of other men even though they are forbidden to do so. The other passages are more troublesome for the opponents of capital punishment, which may explain why one opponent shifts the argument from reliance on the Bible to reliance on Judaism or Jewish law. Jewish law certainly provides for the death penalty. Whoever curses his father or mother is to be stoned, for example, and stoned to death if "he curses them by one of the special names (of God)"; and the law commands a Jew to mourn for deceased relatives, but no mourning is to be observed "for those who have been condemned to death by the court."[7] The argument is made that Jewish law placed so many restrictions on the trial of capital cases that it became "virtually impossible to enforce the death penalty."[8] But virtually impossible is not absolutely impossible. The state of Israel does not authorize capital punishment except—and the law was adopted with the consent of the religious parties—for the likes of Eichmann.

Some Christian writers point to Jesus' declaration that he had not come to abolish the law but to fulfill it,[9] and insist that he amplified his meaning when he added that "whosoever shall kill shall be in danger of the judgment."[10] This, they say, includes the judgment of capital punishment. But the text does not say this. Besides, as opponents of the death penalty say, Christians should forgo quoting "this or that verse," and examine the Bible, and especially the New Testament, for its "total message." Whoever does this cannot fail to see the call for love, for a compassionate concern with the lives of our fellow human beings. As Jesus said: "Thou shalt love the Lord thy God with all thy heart, and with all thy soul, and with all thy mind. This is the first and great commandment. And the second is like unto it, Thou shalt love thy neighbor as thyself."[11] It is argued that the Christian who follows this commandment and models his life on the life of Jesus will purge his heart of all thoughts of vengeance and will ask himself, "What can be done, if anything, to redeem this man and to restore his maimed or brutalized humanity?" The Christian will know that "Cain as well as Abel is made in the image of God," and, rather than put them to death, Christian nations will design correctional institutions whose purpose is to reform or redeem the Cains among them.[12]

Yet, Christian churchmen, even in our own time, are divided on capital punishment. Asked by a British royal commission to express the views of the church, Dr. William Temple, archbishop of Canterbury, said Christians must oppose it, unless an overwhelming case can be made out for its power to deter the commission of murders, and this he doubted; but his successor, Dr. Geoffrey Fisher, said it was a question that each man must decide for himself; the Bible provided no answer.[13] Perhaps we must leave it at that, except to point out that, historically, Christian nations seem to have followed these words of Jesus: "But whoso shall offend one of these little ones which believe in me, it were better for him that a millstone were hanged around his neck, and that he were drowned in the depth of the sea." Then, in a passage that Abraham Lincoln was to quote in

14

his Second Inaugural: "Woe unto the world because of offences! for it must needs be that offences come; but woe to that man by whom the offence cometh!"[14] Christian nations have not hesitated to be the agents by which those who offend against those who believe in Him are hanged by the neck, burned at the stake, broken on a wheel, or (although not so frequently) drowned in the depth of the sea. In fact, the first avowed and forthright argument against the death penalty was written by a man who was horrified by the legal practices of Christian nations. Opposition to capital punishment was born out of liberalism, and liberalism was born in the seventeenth century in reaction to the politics of nominally Christian Europe and, especially, nominally Christian Britain.

The civil war there began when Charles I and Archbishop Laud tried to force episcopacy and the Book of Common Prayer on the Scots; both Charles and Laud were to lose their heads when they lost the war they had begun, and the men who executed them were pious Christians. From among them, or representing only too well one aspect of their souls, came Titus Oates, who told stories about Popish plots. They were false stories, but many a Roman Catholic was hanged because Oates told them before public officials and was believed. Within a few years he himself was to suffer horribly for his false testimony. Since his offense was not a felony in the eyes of the law but only a misdemeanor, Oates could not be sentenced to death; instead, he was pilloried, whipped from Aldgate to Newgate, then, after a two-day interval, whipped again—1,700 times, according to someone who counted—from Newgate to Tyburn. Miraculously, he survived this punishment and was imprisoned. Those who governed at that time were ruled by terrible passions. Even the purest and most moderate of men became their victims: Richard Baxter, for example. Baxter had been a chaplain in the Parliamentary Army, yet he concurred in the Restoration that brought Charles II to the throne; Charles even offered to make him a bishop. But he complained of the perse-

15

cution suffered by the Dissenters, and for this he was brought to trial by James, Charles's brother and successor. To defend Dissenters who had been persecuted for not using the Prayer Book was itself a crime, a libel on the Church of England. He was tried before the chief justice, George Jeffreys by name, and denounced as a rogue, a schismatical knave, and a hypocritical villain who hated the Liturgy and "would have nothing but long-winded cant without book." He was of course convicted. At the same time James's Scottish parliament enacted a law that punished with death anyone who "should preach a conventicle under a roof, or should attend, either as a preacher or as hearer, a conventicle in the open air." Men and women were put to death simply for refusing to renounce their religion and attend Episcopal services. Here is Macaulay's account of the deaths of two Scotswomen, Margaret Maclachlan and Margaret Wilson, the former an aged widow and the latter a girl of eighteen:

They were offered their lives if they would consent to abjure the cause of the insurgent Covenanters, and to attend the Episcopal worship. They refused; and they were sentenced to be drowned. They were carried to a spot which the Solway overflows twice a day, and were fastened to stakes fixed in the sand, between high and low water mark. The elder sufferer was placed near to the advancing flood, in the hope that her last agonies might terrify the younger into submission. The sight was dreadful. But the courage of the survivor was sustained by an enthusiasm as lofty as any that is recorded in martyrology. She saw the sea draw nearer and nearer, but gave no sign of alarm. She prayed and sang verses of psalms till the waves choked her voice. When she had tasted the bitterness of death she was, by a cruel mercy, unbound and restored to life. When she came to herself, pitying friends and neighbours implored her to yield. "Dear Margaret, only say, God save the King!" The poor girl, true to her stern theology, gasped out, "May God save him, if it be God's will!" Her friends crowded round the presiding officer. "She has said it; indeed, Sir, she has said it." "Will she take the abjuration?" he demanded. "Never!" she exclaimed. "I am Christ's; let me go!" And the waters closed over her for the last time.[15]

In the same year, 1685, Richard Rumbold, sentenced to be hanged and quartered for his part in the earl of Argyle's rebellion against James, stood under the gibbet and, although too weak to stand unaided, summoned enough strength to denounce popery and tyranny and to utter words that Jefferson would later paraphrase and make famous in America: "He was a friend, he said, to limited monarchy. But he never would believe that Providence had sent a few men into the world ready booted and spurred to ride, and millions ready saddled and bridled to be ridden"—to which Jefferson appended, "by the Grace of God."[16] Macaulay's summary statement on all this deserves to be quoted:

From the commencement of the civil troubles of the seventeenth century down to the Revolution [of 1688], every victory gained by either party had been followed by a sanguinary proscription. When the Roundheads triumphed over the Cavaliers, when the Cavaliers triumphed over the Roundheads, when the fable of the Popish plot gave the ascendency to the Whigs, when the detection of the Rye House Plot transferred the ascendency to the Tories, blood, and more blood, and still more blood had flowed. Every great explosion and every great recoil of public feeling had been accompanied by severities which, at the time, the predominant faction loudly applauded, but which, on a calm review, history and posterity have condemned.[17]

It is not strange that Thomas Hobbes and John Locke, who lived through much of this time, sought a new foundation for politics and found it in the rights of man, or that the first and most famous opponent of capital punishment was a Hobbesian. Perhaps the most telling argument against a biblical case for abolishing capital punishment is to be found in the actual practice of those countries that claimed to be governed by principles derived from the Bible; and it is not insignificant that the biblical argument does not appear until these countries had been refounded on other principles, principles that are profoundly antibiblical. Opposition to capital punishment is a species of liberalism, but the original thrust of liberalism was liberty against theologically excessive regimes. Liberals were usually anti-Christian. There is, therefore, some reason to believe that those who rely on the Bible to make a case against capital punishment are persuaded of its illegality, impropriety, or unnecessity mainly by other considerations.

THE NATURAL PUBLIC LAW ARGUMENT

The campaign to abolish the death penalty was begun only in 1764 by Cesare Beccaria in one chapter of his unusually influential book, *On Crimes and Punishments*. With its publication, Beccaria achieved instant fame, being hailed throughout Europe, invited to Paris by the Abbé Morellet, and praised by Voltaire as the first man to apply the principles of the new physical and moral sciences—the principles of the Enlightenment—to crime and its treatment.

His reforms required much more than a revision of a criminal code; they required a new order of state, a state founded on new principles, and a state from which the church's influence would be excluded. There are three classes of virtue and vice according to Beccaria: the religious, which are derived from revelation; the natural, which are derived from natural law; and the political, or conventional, which are derived "from the expressed or tacit compacts of men."[18] They need not be in contradiction, he says, but what is derived from one need not be derived from another; and, more to the point he is about to make, what is enjoined by one is not necessarily enjoined by the others. His point is that the law should enjoin only what is derived from the third, "the expressed or tacit compacts of men," and he thinks that enlightened men will not make a tacit compact ratifying all the laws of Moses, for example. He makes an effort to conceal the implications of this, and thereby to avoid proscription by the church, by disingenuously declaring that since he is going to speak only of the third class of virtues and vices, he cannot be said to adopt principles "contrary either to natural law or revelation";[19] but of course the church was not deceived and would have been unusually obtuse to have been deceived. In a later chapter Beccaria says the laws, and only the laws, form "the basis of human morality."[20] Wise governments do not punish "wholly imaginary crimes," but neither do they tolerate "fanatical sermons" that disturb the public tranquillity. Wise governments allow citizens to do anything "that is not contrary to the laws, without having to fear any other inconvenience than that which may result from the action itself"; the laws of a just state will be built on self-interest, the only solid foundation, and not on false opinions or the false idea of utility that causes men to ignore present interests "in order to strengthen distant ones." In fact, the wise government will see to it that men will not be distracted by imaginary things, because the "more respect men have for things beyond the laws, the less can they have for the laws themselves." This, he says, is a principle from which the "wise administrator of public happiness may draw useful consequences"; and he adds coyly that he would expound them himself, except that this would take him "too far from [his] subject." But his meaning is clear enough without this further exposition; as he says in his penultimate chapter, the laws should not be concerned with "indifferent acts"—chief among which is heresy, which he disguises behind the label "a particular kind of crime." The wise government will not punish its Margaret Maclachlans and Margaret Wilsons. By teaching its citizens to "fear the laws and fear nothing else," it will rid itself of those who would punish these religious enthusiasts and, indeed, rid itself of the religious enthusiasts. In a word, *On Crimes and Punishments* calls for the liberal state, and the liberal state requires, to use the term made popular in our day, a massive decriminalization.[21] The church put the book on the *Index Librorum Prohibitorum.*

In the preface, or epistle dedicatory, to the second edition of the book, Beccaria complains that a good part of Europe in the eighteenth century was still living under laws that were "the dregs of utterly barbarous centuries" and were unfit for the men of his time. They ought to avail themselves of the scientific discoveries that had recently been made, specifically of the discoveries made by the new political science, which is a science of sovereignty and the powers appropriate to it. The natural condition of men is one of complete liberty, but it is a liberty "rendered useless by the uncertainty of preserving it" in the state of nature, which, he says echoing Hobbes, is "a continual state of war."[22] To preserve as much of it as possible, men sacrifice a portion of their liberty to the sovereign power they create by their agreement one with another and endow this sovereign with powers, including the power to make laws and to punish their infractions.

He begins his chapter on the death penalty by denying that the sovereign is endowed with the power to impose the punishment of death, and here he departs radically from Hobbes.[23] "What manner of right," he asks, "can men attribute to themselves to slaughter their fellow beings?" None at all, he answers; certainly none that derives from the contract "from which sovereignty and the laws derive." From this contract, or the agreement each man makes with the others to yield a portion of his natural liberty, comes the general will, and the general will is nothing but the "aggregate of particular wills." And there never was a man "who can have wished to leave to other men the choice of killing him." Such a power was never handed over to the sovereign; it could not be handed over to the sovereign because no man has the power in the first place, he says. No man is entitled to take his own life; therefore, he cannot entitle another to take it from him, or for him.[24]

This legal, or natural public law,* argument provoked a re-

*Natural public law is the doctrine according to which rights are assigned to the "sovereign" on the basis of natural law, and this assignment is understood

sponse by a famous public law philosopher, Immanuel Kant, in the first part of his *Metaphysic of Morals:*

. . . . the Marquis of Beccaria, moved by sympathetic sentimentality and an affectation of humanitarianism, has asserted that all capital punishment is illegitimate. He argues that it could not be in the original civil contract, inasmuch as this would imply that every one of the people has agreed to forfeit his life if he murders another (of the people); but such an agreement would be impossible, for no one can dispose of his own life.[25]

But, Kant continues, no one suffers punishment because he has willed it; it is impossible to will to be punished because if what happens to someone is "willed" by him, it cannot be a punishment. What the criminal wills is the punishable action, that is, the crime he voluntarily commits. Beccaria confuses this person who, as subject, is punishable by the penal law, with the juridical person who, as a legislator, or "colegislator," is author of the penal law. These are two persons, Kant says, and Beccaria confuses them. The person who gives himself laws is not the same person who obeys them.

Still, if we ignore the Kantian perspective in which it is appropriate to speak of the two persons of man, and return to the Hobbesian perspective in which Beccaria wrote, we must concede that Beccaria is not altogether wrong to insist that there is no right in the sovereign to take a citizen's life. If civil society is founded on the natural right of self-preservation, it can "hardly demand from the individual that he resign that right . . . by submitting to capital punishment," as Leo Strauss puts it.[26] Hobbes concedes as much when he says that a man who is justly and legally condemned to death nevertheless retains the right to defend himself; indeed, he retains the right to kill his guards or anyone else who would prevent him from escaping.[27] In conceding this, Hobbes admits that there is an insolu-

---

to be valid or legitimate regardless of time or place. See Leo Strauss, *Natural Right and History* (Chicago: The University of Chicago Press, 1953), pp. 190–91.

ble conflict between the right of the sovereign (who represents the will of all) and the natural right of the individual to self-preservation. "This conflict," Strauss says, "was solved in the spirit, if against the letter, of Hobbes by Beccaria, who inferred from the absolute primacy of the right of self-preservation the necessity of abolishing capital punishment."[28] It was solved against the letter of Locke: "Political power, then, I take to be a right of making laws with penalties of death, and consequently all less penalties."[29] It was solved against the letter of Jean-Jacques Rousseau: "How can individuals, who have no right whatever to dispose of their own lives, yet convey this non-existent right to the sovereign?" He answers that the question "looks difficult only because it is badly put." His answer to the question correctly put is that the purpose of the social contract is the preservation of the contracting parties, and he "who wills this end wills the means also."[30] It was solved against the letter of the baron de Montesquieu, whom Beccaria acknowledges to be one of his teachers: "But in moderate governments . . . no man is bereft of life till his very country has attacked him—an attack that is never made without leaving him all possible means of making his defence."[31] It was solved against the letter of even John Stuart Mill, one of the great names in the liberal tradition to which Beccaria belongs.[32] Indeed, no political philosopher before or after Beccaria, with the qualified exception of Jeremy Bentham,[33] has opposed the death penalty as such, although some have opposed its imposition for some (in fact, for most) crimes.*

*Marc Ancel in "The Problem of the Death Penalty," in Sellin, *Capital Punishment* (New York: Harper & Row, 1967), p. 257, claims that Thomas More, in his *Utopia,* opposes the death penalty. He is mistaken. *Utopia* is a dialogue and, like those of Plato's on which it is modeled, it is made up of speeches by characters and in specific settings. The argument against the death penalty is advanced in Book 1 by the character Raphael to an English lawyer and in the presence of a cardinal of the church, the archbishop of Canterbury. Without at all entering into More's meaning, it is enough to say that Raphael, a few pages later in Book 1, praises the penal laws he observed in the country of the "Polyerits," and these laws imposed the death penalty for various crimes. In Book 2, Raphael describes the laws and the "wise and good constitution" of the

Rather than to rely on biblical exegesis, Beccaria would abolish capital punishment by building a political order that does not recognize the relevance of the Bible and, not to speak periphrastically, derives from principles that are incompatible with the Bible. Like the man who established the tradition of which he is a part, Beccaria recognizes that life in the preliberal state, like life in the state of nature, is only too likely to be "solitary, poor, nasty, brutish, and short." Whether paradoxical or only seemingly so, the politics of nominally Christian Europe was not one of peace, love or compassion; on the contrary, it was a politics of crusades, religious wars, and religious civil wars, of persecution, proscription, and banishment, of hanging, drawing, and quartering. It was a politics not of love—it made a mockery of Christ's admonition to love one's neighbors as oneself—but of hate; it bred not heroes but martyrs and their complements, tyrants. In men like Titus Oates and George Jeffreys, who bragged that he had hanged more traitors than all his judicial predecessors together, it inspired and used the meanest and ugliest of the passions. "Dost thou believe that there is a God?" Jeffreys asked Alice Lisle, "Dost thou believe in hell fire? . . . Show me a Presbyterian, and I'll show thee a lying knave. . . . Oh blessed Jesus! What a generation of vipers do we live among!" Let the prisoner be burned alive that very afternoon. All this from the bench, from the chief justice who was soon to become lord chancellor, the highest law officer of the realm. No wonder men were led to seek relief in a politics that made self-preservation the first of the rights of man. Thorsten Sellin recognizes the role played in this by Beccaria when he says that "since the publication of *Crimes and Punishments,* the struggle about [the death penalty] has been one between ancient and

---

Utopians, among whom, he says, he lived for five years. Those laws prescribe, for example, that those who are guilty of adultery and, having been pardoned by the prince, relapse, "are punished with death." More's teaching cannot be understood from these speeches alone, but if Ancel refers to one speech, he is obliged to take account of the speeches that contradict that one.

deeply rooted beliefs in retribution, atonement or vengeance on the one hand, and, on the other, beliefs in the personal value and dignity of the common man."[34]

THE ARGUMENT RESPECTING THE DIGNITY OF MAN

Beccaria deplored the impression caused by the spectacle that attended public executions; a barbaric practice, it could only provide an example of barbarity made more pernicious by clothing it in the formalities and solemnities of law. This was proved by the behavior of the mobs witnessing the spectacle, but nothing said by Beccaria in his thematic treatment of the subject approaches the description provided by Bernard Mandeville, writing in 1725, of the scene attending the progression of the condemned man from Newgate to Tyburn, the place of execution in London:

At last, out they set; and with them a Torrent of Mob bursts through the Gate. Amongst the lower Rank, and working People, the idlest, and such as are most fond of making Holidays, with Prentices and Journeymen to the meanest Trades, are the most honourable Part of these floating Multitudes. All the rest are worse. The Days being known before-hand, they are a Summons to all Thieves and Pickpockets, of both Sexes, to meet. Great Mobs are a Safeguard to one another, which makes these Days Jubilees, on which old Offenders, and all who dare not shew their Heads on any other, venture out of their Holes; and they resemble Free Marts, where there is an Amnesty for all Outlaws. All the way, from *Newgate* to *Tyburn,* is one continued Fair, for Whores and Rogues of the meaner Sort. Here the most abandon'd Rakehells may light on Women as shameless: Here Trollops, all in Rags, may pick up Sweethearts of the same Politeness: And there are none so lewd, so vile, or so indigent, of either Sex, but at the Time and Place aforesaid, they may find a Paramour. . . . Now you see a Man, without Provocation, push his Companion in the Kennel; and two Minutes after, the Sufferer trip up the other's Heels, and the first Aggressor lies rolling

24

in the more solid Mire: And he is the prettiest Fellow among them, who is the least shock'd at Nastiness, and the most boisterous in his Sports.[35]

Such a scene—and this is only a sample of Mandeville's description—is a travesty of the law and its putative purposes: the most debased citizens disporting themselves on the occasion of the killing of one of them, while he, fortified by liquor, strikes a pose of false courage, shaking their hands and joining in their revelry. It would be hard to imagine a more inhuman scene, or one so lacking in the dignity that ought to attend human affairs —and all this promoted by the offices of law. It is not by chance that in the course of time it became necessary to hide executions from the public's eye. Men cannot witness the lopping off of heads or the breaking or stretching of necks without becoming less human as a result. What, asks Beccaria, are the sentiments of each and every man about the death penalty? "Let us read them in the acts of indignation and contempt with which everyone regards the hangman."[36] It was an outraged public that, in our own time, finally succeeded in forcing the authorities to conceal the hangman and his work behind the forbidding walls of institutions; however, the effect of this concealment was to prolong the practice of capital punishment.

Albert Camus makes much of this point. Not only do modern Western societies conceal their executions behind walls, but they conceal the horror of executions behind the euphemisms employed to describe the practice and its victims. They speak of the "condemned paying his debt to society" and refer to him as the "patient" or the "interested party." In this way words are emptied of their meaning and the imagination allowed to sleep. "But if people are shown the machine [the guillotine], made to touch the wood and steel and hear the sound of a head falling, then public imagination, suddenly awakened, will repudiate both the vocabulary and the [death] penalty."[37] To the extent that this is possible, his words force us to touch that wood and steel and hear that sound. Consider:

Instead of vaguely evoking a debt that someone this very morning paid society, would it not be a more effective example to remind each taxpayer in detail of what he may expect? Instead of saying: "If you kill, you will atone for it on the scaffold," wouldn't it be better to tell him, for purposes of example: "If you kill, you will be imprisoned for months or years, torn between an impossible despair and a constantly renewed terror, until one morning we shall slip into your cell after removing our shoes the better to take you by surprise while you are sound asleep after the night's anguish. We shall fall on you, tie your hands behind your back, cut with scissors your shirt collar and your hair if need be. Perfectionists that we are, we shall bind your arms with a strap so that you are forced to stoop and your neck will be more accessible. Then we shall carry you, an assistant on each side supporting you by the arm, with your feet dragging behind through the corridors. Then, under a night sky, one of the executioners will finally seize you by the seat of your pants and throw you horizontally on a board while another will steady your head in the lunette and a third will let fall from a height of seven feet a hundred-and-twenty-pound blade that will slice off your head like a razor."[38]

He then insists that we read the testimony of attending physicians as to the flow of blood, the contraction and fibrillation of the muscles, and even the blinking of an eye in a severed head. His purpose is not to recreate the sort of debasement that characterized the executions at Tyburn, but rather, by appealing to our most humane sentiments, to cause us to blanch at the sight of cruelty, to see the penalty of death for what it is, and thereby to hasten the day of its abolition. He would have the French government erect the guillotine on a platform in the Place de la Concorde, invite the public as witnesses, and televize the ceremony for the benefit of those who cannot attend in person. Then the public, made more gentle by life under the liberal and liberalizing regimes that have governed Western men since the days of Tyburn, will demand abolition of the practice; then the public will reject the counsel of the "retentionists," whom Arthur Koestler calls the "hang-hards," whose appeal is only to "ignorance, traditional prejudice and repressed cruelty."[39] Capital punishment, it is said, has always been associated with barbarism, and when it is exhibited to the civilized men of our time, they will abolish it as inconsistent with their ideas of "the sanctity of life, the dignity of man, and a humane criminal law."[40] They will, with Koestler, see the gallows as not merely a machine of death but "the oldest and most obscene symbol of that tendency in mankind which drives it towards moral self-destruction."[41]

It is necessary that the U.S. Constitution forbid the infliction of cruel and unusual punishments; such a provision is required by the principles on which the country was built. Liberalism aimed at the relief of man's estate on this earth—not the estate of one man or the estates of a favored class, but of all men— and it required a greater respect for individual autonomy and, it is insisted, dignity. The establishment of the United States was a milestone in the growing civilization of the world; as the motto on its Great Seal still proclaims, it was a *novus ordo seclorum*, a new order of the ages, and, as such, it would, because it must, abolish all traces of the barbarism that in the past disgraced too many lands. The barbaric punishments of the past—"punishments which inflict torture, such as the rack, the thumbscrew, the iron boot, the stretching of limbs, and the like"[42]—are not only painful but, as Justice William J. Brennan, Jr., points out, to be condemned because "they treat members of the human race as nonhumans, as objects to be toyed with and discarded." They are, therefore, cruel and unusual in the sense of the constitutional clause because that clause recognizes "that even the vilest criminal remains a human being possessed of common human dignity."[43] It grants no leave to the terrible desire to inflict pain or to witness the torments suffered by other human beings; it forbids punishments that are degrading to the dignity of human beings, degrading both to those who suffer them and to those who inflict and witness them. And it is insisted that the penalty of death belongs in this category of forbidden punishments, for, whatever the method of execution, it degrades victim and executioner alike. What sort of person willingly chooses to be the hangman? Who, in our day, willingly chooses to witness the performance of his grisly work?

Who opposes the death penalty in our day? The answer given is eminent jurists, criminologists, theologians, academicians of a variety of disciplines, world famous men of letters, and the ACLU, the Legal Defense Fund of the National Association for the Advancement of Colored People, the American Society for the Abolition of Capital Punishment, and Citizens Against Legalized Murder, Inc.[44] Who, in our day, favors it? The answer given is the brutes, the ignorant, and the fearful. To favor it is to reveal "doctrinaire, dogmatic, unempirical, and irrational convictions immune to any argument."[45] This, it is said, is characteristic of the police who insist that, however harsh or even inhumane, it is the only punishment capable of deterring murder.

THE DETERRENCE ARGUMENT

The purpose of punishment, according to Beccaria, "can only be to prevent the criminal from inflicting new injuries on . . . citizens and to deter others from similar acts."[46] Incapacitation and deterrence are the ends, and, to the extent possible, mildness should characterize the means of achieving them. Severity —or, as he puts it in the following chapter, "gradations of intensity" beyond what is needed "to deter men from committing crimes"—is unjust. Beccaria is of the opinion that, on the whole, criminals can be deterred by the threat of punishments much milder than those being imposed. The death penalty, which was imposed for a variety of crimes, was unnecessary, in his opinion, even for the most awful of them. A long prison sentence—if necessary, a "whole lifetime . . . spent in servitude and pain"—is sufficient to deter, and what is sufficient to deter and no more is just. Unable to *prove* that imprisonment is a sufficient deterrent, since he was writing long before the time of empirical social science, he points to countries where, for a time, the death penalty was not imposed, and he was satisfied that the murder rate had not increased there. In this fashion, Beccaria originated the most frequently used argument against the death penalty, namely, that it is unnecessary.

He did not begin with this argument, he began with the argument that civil society was not authorized to take human life. But he used it to buttress his case. In itself the argument is not compelling, because a practice might be unnecessary and yet be innocuous, but when combined with the argument concerning the illegality of the death penalty, it acquires considerable force. Police are employed to prevent the commission of crimes and to catch criminals, and if prosecutors, criminal trials, prisons, and executions are employed only to prevent further offenses by those we catch up in this system and to deter others, and if these purposes can be as readily accomplished by prison terms as by executions, then the case for abolition would seem to have been made. So in our day the abolitionists do not begin with the deterrence argument, but resort to it in order to meet the assertion of the "retentionists" that death is the only penalty sufficient to deter heinous crimes, especially murder. If this can be shown to be untrue, the case against abolition would seem to have been destroyed. The abolitionists have devoted a good deal of energy to the task of demonstrating that the death penalty is unnecessary, of showing that it has no differential effect as a deterrent when weighed against the possible alternatives, such as life imprisonment.

Most students of the question have been persuaded by social science studies that "the ineffectiveness of the death penalty as a deterrent to murder has been demonstrated convincingly."[47] The point is made that the rate of homicides varies from place to place and from time to time, but that the imposition of the death penalty rather than a long-term prison sentence is not a factor in these variations, or, at a minimum, has not been shown to be a factor. To this the abolitionists have testified in hearing after hearing, trial after trial, and investigation after investigation. In what is surely the most influential study of deterrence, a study cited favorably by a number of governmental commissions here and abroad, Thorsten Sellin compares the homicide rates in contiguous states and finds no significant differences among them in the number of homicides per 100,000 population whether they have the death penalty or not. He then examines the murder rate within single states before and after abolition of the death penalty, and again finds no difference. He concludes that "the death penalty, as we use it, exercises no influence on the extent or fluctuating rates of capital crimes."[48] Other social scientists have found similar results. They have tested the retentionists' proposition that the death penalty is a superior deterrent to life imprisonment for criminal homicide, and, even if it cannot be said that the proposition has been disproved, it can be said that it has not been confirmed; in fact, one authority insists that it has been "disconfirmed" by the uniformity or consistency of the findings published.[49] This is sufficient to support their case for abolition: to deter criminal homicide it is not necessary to resort to this ancient and barbaric practice. Nevertheless, it bears repeating that however much the modern debate on capital punishment has focused on the deterrence issue, the abolitionists do not rest their case on their finding that it has no differential deterrence capacity. Victor Gollancz makes this point as well as any of them:

> If I believed the opposite of what I do believe; if I believed it established, beyond the possibility of a doubt, that the death penalty is preventive of murder as nothing else could be; if—I am anxious to put my case in as extreme a form as possible, so that nobody can misunderstand me—if I felt certain that abolition would immediately be followed by a startling increase in the numbers of murders: I should still say, and say with undiminished conviction, that the most urgent of all tasks which confront us, or could confront any people that had a care for religious or humane values, is the ending of capital punishment.[50]

THE CONSTITUTIONAL ARGUMENT

We Americans have debated the morality and necessity of the death penalty throughout almost the entire period of our experience as a nation, and, until 1976 when the Supreme Court ruled in favor of its constitutionality,[51] it had been debated among us in constitutional terms, which is not true elsewhere. The Eighth Amendment clearly and expressly forbids the imposition of "cruel and unusual punishments," a prohibition that applies now to the states as well as to the national government; it was argued that the death penalty was such a punishment.

It is, of course, incontestable that the death penalty was not regarded as cruel and unusual by the men who wrote and ratified the amendment. They may have forbidden cruel and unusual punishments but they acknowledged the legitimacy of capital punishment when, in the Fifth Amendment, they provided that no person "shall be held to answer for a capital . . . crime, unless on a presentment or indictment of a Grand Jury," and when in the same amendment they provided that no one shall, for the same offense, "be twice put in jeopardy of life or limb," and when, in the Fifth as well as in the Fourteenth Amendment, they forbade, not the taking of life, but the taking of life "without due process of law." We also know that the same Congress which proposed the Eighth Amendment also provided for the death penalty in the first Crimes Act.[52] Even Thomas Jefferson favored the death penalty for murder and treason,[53] and George Washington, despite powerful entreaties, could not be persuaded to commute the death sentence imposed on Major John André, the British officer and spy involved in Benedict Arnold's treachery. So the death penalty can be held to be cruel and unusual in the constitutional sense only if it has somehow become so in the passage of time.

31

Until recently the Supreme Court had invalidated punishments under this clause only on the ground of inappropriateness: in 1910, the Court held it to be inappropriate and therefore cruel to sentence a man convicted of fraudulent practices to fifteen years imprisonment at hard labor, to be chained, wrist to ankle, during twelve years of this sentence, and to be permanently deprived of some of his civil rights.[54] In a sense, this means that the Eighth Amendment requires the punishment to fit the crime. But this is not the only respect in which a punishment may be cruel and unusual: some punishments are intrinsically so, irrespective of the crimes for which they are inflicted, and would have been so regarded by the authors of the amendment. Drawing and quartering and disemboweling serve as examples of such punishments. But the fact that such punishments were once usual shows that opinions of cruel and unusual vary from place to place and time to time. A practice that was once acceptable even in America—ear-cropping comes to mind—is probably unacceptable today. In 1958 the Supreme Court recognized this when it held loss of citizenship to be a cruel and unusual punishment.[55] Not only did it so hold, but it said that the meaning of cruel and unusual depends on "the evolving standards of decency that mark the progress of a maturing society." Surely, it is argued, hanging or electrocution or gassing is, in our day, regarded as equally cruel as expatriation, if not more cruel.[56] Is it not relevant that the American people have insisted that executions be carried out by more humane methods, that they not be carried out in public, and that the penalty be imposed for fewer and fewer crimes; and is it not significant that juries have shown a tendency to refuse to convict for capital crimes? In these ways the people are merely demonstrating what has been true for centuries, namely, that when given the opportunity to act, the average man (as opposed to judges and vindictive politicians)[57] will refuse to be a party to legal murder.

One of the familiar facts about English juries during the

period when the death sentence was mandatory for scores of felonies was their tendency to go to great lengths to avoid having to convict for a capital crime. If, for example, it was a capital crime to steal property valued at forty or more shillings, many a jury solemnly and shamelessly set a value of thirty-nine shillings on property worth much more. The willingness to accept a defense of insanity is merely one of the ways modern juries accomplish the same end. Perhaps the most interesting illustration of this uneasiness in the face of the death penalty is the ancient privilege of benefit of clergy. This privilege had a history in England that extended from the earliest time for which we have records up to the year 1827, when it was finally abolished by act of Parliament. At the time it originated, all felonies except petty larceny and mayhem carried the death penalty at common law, but clerics in orders could be tried only in ecclesiastical courts which were not authorized to impose the death penalty for any offense. In the course of centuries, not merely the clergy—the *habitum et tonsuram clericalem*—but their lay assistants and then anyone who could read and finally, in the eighteenth century, everyone, was eligible to claim the privilege. As might be expected, this development was paralleled by another according to which more and more offenses were made "nonclergyable"; still, throughout most of English history "benefit of clergy" served to moderate the common law's excessively sanguinary schedule of punishments.[58]

The fact of the matter, or so it is alleged, is that American juries have shown an increasing tendency to avoid imposing the death penalty except on certain offenders who are distinguished not by their criminality but by their race or class. Justice Douglas emphasized this in his opinion in the 1972 capital punishment cases. "One searches our chronicles in vain for the execution of any members of the affluent strata of this society," he said. "The Leopolds and Loebs are given prison terms, not sentenced to death."[59] The facts in those cases seem to bear him out. William Furman entered a private house at about two A.M.

intending to burglarize it. He was carrying a gun. When heard by the head of the household, William Micke, a father of five children, Furman attempted to flee the house. Unfortunately, he tripped over something on the back porch and his gun discharged, hitting Micke through a closed door and killing him. He was quickly apprehended, then tried and convicted. The statute under which he was convicted authorized but did not mandate the death penalty when the killing occurred in the course of committing a felony; the jury, empowered to choose between death and life imprisonment, chose death. In the second case, Lucius Jackson, an escaped convict, entered the house of a twenty-one-year-old woman after her husband had left for work. Discovered by her hiding in her baby's closet, he threatened her with a scissors and demanded money. A struggle ensued. Holding the scissors to her throat, Jackson then raped her. Georgia law at this time, 1968, permitted the jury to choose between the death penalty, life imprisonment, or "imprisonment and labor in the penitentiary for not less than one year nor more than 20 years." The jury chose death. In the third case, Elmer Branch, a twenty-year-old Texan, entered the house of a sixty-five-year-old widow while she was asleep; holding his arm against her throat, he raped her, then stole what little money he was able to find in the house. Texas law provided that a person convicted of rape should be punished by death, life imprisonment, or imprisonment "for any term of years not less than five." Once again, the jury chose to impose the death penalty. Such are the facts in these three cases that reached the Supreme Court in 1972. In the light of the sentences imposed, however, the salient facts were these: all three offenders were black and all three victims were white. Death sentences are imposed not out of a hatred of the crimes committed, it is said, but out of a hatred of blacks. Of the 3,859 persons executed in the United States in the period 1930–1967, 2,066, or 54 percent, were black.[60] More than half of the prisoners now under sentence of death are black. In short, the death penalty, we have been told, "may have served" to keep blacks, especially southern blacks, "in a position of subjugation and subservience."[61] That in itself is unconstitutional.

CONCLUSION

In the 1972 cases only two of the nine justices of the Supreme Court argued that the death penalty as such is a violation of the Eighth Amendment, regardless of the manner of its imposition. Justice Brennan was persuaded by what he saw as the public's growing reluctance to impose it that the rejection of the death penalty "could hardly be more complete without becoming absolute."[62] Yet, on the basis of his own evidence it is clear that the American people have not been persuaded by the arguments against the death penalty and that they continue to support it for *some* criminals—so long as it is carried out privately and as painlessly as possible. At the very time he was writing there were more than 600 persons on whom Americans had imposed the sentence of death. He drew the conclusion that the American people had decided that capital punishment does not comport with human dignity and is therefore unconstitutional, but the facts he cited do not support this conclusion. This may explain why his colleague, Justice Marshall, felt obliged to take up the argument.

Marshall acknowledged that the public opinion polls show that, on the whole, capital punishment is supported by a majority of the American people,[63] but he denied the validity—or the "utility"—of ascertaining opinion on this subject by simply polling the people. The polls ask the wrong question. It is not a question of whether the public accepts the death penalty, but

35

whether the public when "fully informed as to the purposes of the penalty and its liabilities would find [it] shocking, unjust, and unacceptable."

> In other words, the question with which we must deal is not whether a substantial proportion of American citizens would today, if polled, opine that capital punishment is barbarously cruel, but whether they would find it to be so in the light of all information presently available.[64]

This information, he said, "would almost surely convince the average citizen that the death penalty was unwise."[65] He conceded that this citizen might nevertheless support it as a way of exacting retribution, but, in his view, the Eighth Amendment forbids "punishment for the sake of retribution";[66] besides, he said, no one has ever seriously defended capital punishment on retributive grounds. It has been defended only with "deterrent or other similar theories." From here he reached his conclusion that "the great mass of citizens" would decide that the death penalty is not merely unwise but also "immoral and therefore unconstitutional." They would do so if they knew what he knew, and what he knew was that retribution is illegitimate and unconstitutional and that the death penalty is excessive and unnecessary, being no more capable than life imprisonment of deterring the crimes for which it is imposed. He conceded that the evidence on the deterrence issue is not "convincing beyond all doubt, but it is persuasive."[67] Thus, the death penalty *is* cruel and unusual punishment because the American people *ought* to think so. Shortly after this decision thirty-five states enacted new statutes authorizing the death penalty for certain crimes.

This public support for capital punishment is a puzzling fact, especially in our time. It is a policy that has almost no articulate supporters in the intellectual community. The subject has been vigorously debated and intensively investigated by state after state and country after country—California and Connecticut,

Texas and Wisconsin; Britain and Canada, Ceylon and "Europe"; even the United Nations; and, of course, various committees of the U.S. Congress.[68] Among those willing to testify and publish their views, the abolitionists outweigh the "retentionists" both in number and, with significant exceptions, in the kind of authority that is recognized in the worlds of science and letters. Yet the Harris poll reports 59 percent of the general population to be in favor of capital punishment, and that proportion is increasing—at this time, at least.[69]

Such a phenomenon cannot be attributed to the structure of American society; indeed, there is good reason to believe that in those countries where capital punishment has been abolished by law or allowed to languish in practice, it has been done in the face of evidence showing that the majority of the people favor the penalty. In 1967, Canada, with a population quite similar in the relevant respects to the American, suspended the death penalty for five years (and in 1972 for another five), but this action was taken by a free vote in the House of Commons so that no party could fairly be held responsible for the measure by the voters; and there was considerable public clamor for its reinstitution. It had been retained as a penalty for those convicted of killing policemen and prison guards, but, against the clear wishes of the public, the government commuted the sentences of everyone found guilty of these capital offenses. No one has been executed in Canada since 1962. In 1976, the Parliament adopted legislation abolishing the penalty for all crimes, yet Solicitor General Warren Allmand, the cabinet official in charge of the administration of justice, who said publicly more than once that he would resign rather than sign a death warrant, admitted that a contemporary study commissioned by his office disclosed that 80 percent of a national sample of the population favored capital punishment.[70] Britain abolished it provisionally in 1965 and unconditionally in 1970, but it was done in a private bill and at a time when 79 percent of the British people were in favor of retaining it or "expressed their uncertainty on the abolition question." The bill's sponsor had no illusions about acting with public support; he said that matters of life and death should not be decided on the basis of opinion expressed "on the street corner or in a club or pub."[71] Similarly, in Canada one of the solicitor general's advisers on the issue insisted that "uninformed or irrational public opinion is not a justification for bringing back the noose," and he went on to characterize those who want to bring it back (which is to say, 80 percent of the population) as likely to be "insecure . . . severely brought up, and . . . maladjusted socially."[72]

It is sometimes argued that the opinion polls are deceptive insofar as the question is posed abstractly—and can only be posed abstractly—and that the responses of these publics would be different if they had to decide whether particular persons should be executed. This is entirely possible, or even probable; nevertheless, there is no gainsaying the fact that juries, for whom the issue is very concrete indeed, continue to impose death sentences on a significant number of criminals. Ordinary men and women seem to be unpersuaded by the social science argument against deterrence, or they regard it as irrelevant; they seem to be oblivious to the possibility that innocent people might be executed;[73] they know nothing about the natural public law disagreement between Beccaria and Kant; they surely do not share the opinion that executions are contrary to God's commands; indeed, they seem to display the passions of many a biblical character in their insistence that, quite apart from all these considerations, murderers should be paid back. In fact, the essential difference between the public and the abolitionists is almost never discussed in our time; it has to do with retribution: the public insists on it without using the word and the abolitionists condemn it whenever they mention it.

The abolitionists condemn it because it springs from revenge, they say, and revenge is the ugliest passion in the human soul. They condemn it because it justifies punishment for the sake of punishment alone, and they are opposed to punishment that serves no purpose beyond inflicting pain on its victims. Strictly speaking, they are opposed to punishment. They may, like Beccaria, sometimes speak of life imprisonment as the alternative to executions, but they are not in fact advocates of life imprisonment and will not accept it.[74] Homicide can be deterred by much milder sentences, they say or imply. The 1976 Canadian law calls for mandatory life *sentences* for first-degree murder, but not mandatory life imprisonment; there is the possibility of parole after twenty-five years. Even that was seen as too harsh; another section of the law allows the possibility of parole after fifteen years.

They condemn retribution because they see it, rightly or wrongly, as the only basis on which the death penalty can be supported. To kill an offender is not only unnecessary but precludes the possibility of reforming him, and reformation, they say, is the only civilized response to the criminal. Even murderers—indeed, especially murderers—are capable of being redeemed or of repenting their crimes. Camus tells the story of one Bernard Fallot, a member of a particularly vicious gang that worked for the Gestapo, who admitted having committed many terrible crimes.

Public opinion and the opinion of his judges certainly classed him among the irremediable, and I should have been tempted to agree if I had not read a surprising testimony. This is what Fallot said . . . after declaring that he wanted to die courageously: "Shall I tell you my greatest regret? Well, it is not having known the Bible I now have here. I assure you that I wouldn't be where I now am."[75]

What is accomplished by killing this man? To kill him may satisfy the public's desire to wreak revenge on him, but no good and much harm is accomplished by giving vent to such passions. Besides, to kill him is to waste another valuable human life, a life that in the future would surely be devoted to good works. Not only should he not be killed, he should not be imprisoned. The elimination of capital punishment must be followed by the elimination of all punishment for the sake of punishment alone; only when the law is purged of the punitive spirit can we solve the crime problem.

Though capital punishment was a contradiction to the chosen methods of nineteenth-century penology, which had revolted against violence, that penology still accepted the necessity of exacting retribution from criminals. Present-day penology, by contrast, puts its emphasis not on retribution, nor even on deterrence, but on rehabilitation. It combats crime by such reformative and essentially nonpunitive means as probation and psychiatric help in and out of prisons. It seeks eventually to replace the old concept of "the punishment to fit the crime" with a quite new notion: "the treatment to fit the criminal."[76]

Not even a murderer deserves to be *punished*.

The goal of the abolitionists is not merely the elimination of capital punishment but the reform or rehabilitation of the criminal, *even* if he is a murderer. The public that favors capital punishment is of the opinion that the murderer deserves to be punished, and does not deserve to be treated, even if by treatment he *could* be rehabilitated.

CHAPTER II

The Death Penalty
and the
Spirit of Reform

BECCARIA was the first criminologist, insofar as he was the first man to devote his attention exclusively to the study of crimes and punishments and their reform. He was the first criminologist to argue openly against retribution and to reduce punishment to deterrence, and he is credited with being the first to argue that imprisonment is a proper mode of punishment.[1] It was Beccaria who promised with respect to crime and punishment in particular what the Enlightenment promised in general, a solution to a human problem based on the discoveries and techniques of modern science. As I indicated in the previous chapter, Thorsten Sellin, one of Beccaria's most distinguished successors in the field of criminology, acknowledged his significant contributions to the cause of reform when he described what has happened since Beccaria. Here I quote him in full:

. . . the struggle about [the death penalty] has been one between ancient and deeply rooted beliefs in retribution, atonement or ven-

41

geance on the one hand, and, on the other, beliefs in the personal value and dignity of the common man that were born of the democratic movement of the eighteenth century, as well as beliefs in the scientific approach to an understanding of the motive forces of human conduct, which are the result of the growth of the sciences of behavior during the nineteenth and twentieth centuries. If these newer trends of our thinking continue undisturbed the death penalty will disappear in all the countries of Western culture sooner or later.[2]

Beccaria went to Paris, the acknowledged capital of the Enlightenment and, therefore, of reform; he knew Voltaire, Morellet (who immediately translated his book into French), Denis Diderot, Jean Le Roud d'Alembert, and Paul Henri Dietrich d'Holbach. A young deputy named Maximilien Robespierre was to speak eloquently against the death penalty in the 1791 Constituent Assembly, quoting Beccaria time and again;[3] but, considering the fate of reform in the French Revolution (it suffices to recall the thousands sent to the newly invented guillotine by Robespierre), it was not strange that America should be the place where the principles of the new science of crimes and punishments should first be applied. In a very real sense America was the first new nation. As Alexander Hamilton observed in the first essay of *The Federalist,* it had been "frequently remarked that it seems to have been reserved to the people of this country, by their conduct and example, to decide the important question, whether societies of men are really capable or not of establishing good government from reflection and choice, or whether they are forever destined to depend for their political constitutions on accident and force." The Constitution was ratified, in no small part because of Hamilton's efforts; and whether his doubts were stilled by the success of his advocacy is of no concern to us here. The experiment in self-government was launched, and launched on the principles of the rights of man. There would be no national religious establishment, and Jefferson and Madison especially acted to disestablish the state churches, thus going far to accomplish one condition of Beccaria's "decriminalization." The Fifth Amendment forbade the use of torture, as well as providing other protections for those accused of crimes. The country survived a difficult first decade and the people prospered. It was only to be expected that the American people would set out to correct the wide variety of mistakes made—in many cases, innocently—by their less fortunate predecessors. This "new order of the ages" provided a setting congenial to reform movements and was characterized by great expectations. Americans had built their government itself on the solid foundation provided by the new science of politics, as Hamilton said in the ninth *Federalist,* and some of them were confident that, once they were rid of the prejudices, habits, and "mistaken religious opinions" inherited from a less enlightened age (the phrase is Edward Livingston's, used in his proposed criminal code for Louisiana), they would build a society that would be a model for men everywhere. As David Brion Davis has pointed out,[4] the movement to reform the law of punishments and to abolish the death penalty was only one of the causes that captured the attention and engaged the passions of many Americans during their first years as a nation. Along with it went the antislavery, temperance, and feminist movements, for example, and they were all to flourish and at least one of them to succeed.

THE INVENTION OF THE PENITENTIARY

In the American colonies, as in England, prisons were not understood to be an "ordinary mechanism of correction," as David Rothman puts it;[5] the criminal codes of the eighteenth century provided for fines, whippings, "mechanisms of shame" (stocks, the pillory, and public cages), banishment, and all too frequently the gallows. In prerevolutionary New York, for example, more than 20 percent of all sentences handed down by the Supreme Court were death sentences.[6] Like the English, Americans did not know what to do with their criminals, except to do what they had always done, but earlier than the English they set out to find a better way. A new nation, established on new principles, seemed to be the "ideal place for enacting Beccaria's principles," as William Bradford said in 1793, and he was not alone in thinking the death penalty to be unnecessary in America.[7]

The movement to abolish capital punishment in America and to reform the law of punishment was initiated by Dr. Benjamin Rush in 1787 in a paper delivered in Benjamin Franklin's house in Philadelphia. The reform movement could have begun under more auspicious circumstances, or perhaps it would be more accurate to say, under more favorable auspices, only if it could have attracted the active support of the leading Founders; but these sober men held themselves aloof, perhaps because they thought the constitutional provisions met the case. Still, Rush himself was a signer of the Declaration of Independence, Philadelphia was the city in which the Constitution was written, 1787 was the year in which it was written, and it would be supererogatory to detail Franklin's various contributions to the nation's founding. (Franklin did not, however, favor abolition of the death penalty.)[8]

Philadelphia was also William Penn's "city of brotherly love," the home of the Quakers, inveterate reformers who would not have supported the Constitution without the assurance—privately given[9]—that Congress possessed the authority (after January 1, 1808) to abolish slavery and who made it a practice, beginning with the First Congress, to petition Congress to set about this business. The colony's first constitution, Penn's "Great Act" of 1682, had effected a significant reform of the criminal law by abolishing the death penalty for all crimes except premeditated murder, and it was only at the insistence of the Crown that, on the occasion of Penn's death in 1718, the "intolerant and sanguinary system of the common law of England"[10] was reimposed on the colony. Pennsylvania restored the reform in 1794, after independence, and in the spirit of Penn began the task of reforming the whole of the criminal law.

Rush's first call for abolition of the death penalty was part of "An Enquiry into the Effects of Public Punishments Upon Criminals and Upon Society." In this paper, and even more markedly in his 1794 paper devoted solely to capital punishment, Rush showed the influence of Beccaria. While he did not succeed in having the death penalty abolished for all crimes, his first paper led immediately to the founding of the Philadelphia Society for Alleviating the Miseries of Public Prisons and, in 1790, to the establishment of the world's first penitentiary. Here Beccaria's milder punishment would be inaugurated, and here prisoners would be housed in conditions that met the standards of John Howard, the great English prison reformer. In addition, it was to be a penitentiary, a "house of repentance," as Rush called it, a place "for the cure of the diseases of the mind." With this, the reform movement took on a character that marks it to this day.

The penitentiary was seen as an alternative to the punishments imposed in Britain—death and banishment—as well as to the American practice of inflicting public punishments in the form of the whipping post, the pillory, the stocks, and what Rush saw as degrading public labor. (His particular target was the so-called "wheelbarrow law" which required persons convicted of felonies to perform work on the streets of Philadelphia.) For reasons to be explained shortly, Rush saw the primary purpose of punishment to be reform of the criminal, and quite obviously the penalty of death was least calculated to achieve this. For somewhat similar reasons, he rejected banishment; not only was it "next in degree, in folly and in cruelty, to the punishment of death," but it deprived society of the advantages that derive from a man's love of kindred and country, to Rush a natural passion that could be rekindled in the heart of every criminal. And public punishment, he said, is calculated to have a deleterious effect not only on those who suffer it but on those who observe it.

Reform of the criminal cannot be achieved by subjecting him to public display and disgrace. The infamy attached to it destroys his sense of shame and his reputation, and having lost these, he has nothing left to lose in society; the likely effect is to harden his criminal propensities and to instill in him a desire to revenge himself on the society whose laws subjected him to this treatment. Besides, being usually of short duration, a public punishment produces no changes in body or mind of the sort needed to reform the habits of vice. It is said that public punishment, by striking terror in the hearts of those who observe it, deters them from committing crimes. Not so, says Rush. In the first place, it fosters fortitude in the criminal (and this is said to be especially true in the case of public executions),[11] who is then admired by the crowd, and it goes without saying—for Rush, at least—that criminals should not be admired. But this is only part of the story. The sight of the criminal's suffering is likely to provoke sympathy for him; but, forbidden by the law (and their good character which has been developed by the law) to sympathize with criminals, this sympathy is "rendered abortive," insofar as it is deprived of an object to which it can attach itself. The effect of this—or so Rush maintains—is positively harmful to society. "The principle of sympathy after being often opposed by the law of the state, which forbids it to relieve the distress it commiserates, will cease to act altogether; and from this defect of action, and the habit arising out of it, will soon lose its place in the human breast." People will then come to view with indifference the misery of widows, orphans, the naked and the sick, as well as the misery of prisoners—"and what is worse than all, when [this] the sentinel of our moral faculty is removed, there is nothing to guard the mind from the inroads of every positive vice."[12] This natural sensibility, or natural moral sense, must be kindled and cherished; from it comes the obligation to love "the whole human race"; but the sight of the criminal, instead of exciting pity, may excite indignation and contempt, and this will extinguish a portion of this universal love. And if the sight of the criminal does not provoke contempt—which may be the case with other criminals or with those who are too young or innocent to understand that the punishment follows a crime—his being punished will appear to be an arbitrary act of cruelty. This may lead the observers to commit such acts against their fellow citizens. The effect, then, is to remove "the natural obstacles to violence and murder in the human mind."

The same analysis of the moral sensibilities that condemned public punishments pointed to the solution, punishment inflicted in private:

Let a large house, of a construction agreeable to its design be erected in a remote part of the state. Let the avenue to this house be rendered difficult and gloomy by mountains or morasses. Let its doors be of iron; and let the grating, occasioned by opening and shutting them, be encreased by an echo from a neighboring mountain, that shall extend and continue a sound that shall deeply pierce the soul. Let a guard constantly attend at a gate that shall lead to this place of punishment, to prevent strangers from entering it. Let all the officers of the house be strictly forbidden ever to discover any signs of mirth, or even levity, in the presence of the criminals. To encrease the horror of this abode of discipline and misery, let it be called by some name that shall import its design.[13]

Its remoteness, its forbidding secrecy, the unknown length of time to which criminals were to be confined in it, and the unknown character of the punishments to be inflicted within its walls are best calculated to "diffuse terror thro' a community, and thereby to prevent crimes."

Children will press upon the evening fire in listening to the tales that will be spread from this abode of misery. Superstition will add to its

47

horrors, and romance will find in it ample materials for fiction, which cannot fail of encreasing the terror of its punishments.[14]

It came to be called the penitentiary. Established on the proper principles, it would make other forms of punishment unnecessary; it would not only deter crimes by striking terror in the hearts of the people, but it might also effect the reform of the criminal. Even the crime of murder has its "cure in moral and physical influence." Properly conceived, punishment would consist of "bodily pain, labour, watchfulness, solitude, and silence," in varying degrees appropriate to each class of criminal; but this would be combined with "regular instruction in the principles, and obligations of religion." Prisoners were to be penitents.

The spirit in which these reforms were proposed is nowhere better displayed than in the following sentences:

> If the invention of a machine for facilitating labour, has been repaid with the gratitude of a country, how much more will that man deserve, that shall invent the most speedy and effectual methods of restoring the vicious part of mankind to virtue and happiness, and of extirpating a portion of vice from the world? Happy condition of human affairs! When humanity, philosophy and christianity, shall unite their influence to teach men, that they are bretheren; and to prevent their preying any longer upon each other! Happy citizens of the United States, *whose governments permit them to adopt every discovery in the moral and intellectual world,* that leads to these benevolent purposes![15]

In America, science and government were not enemies, but friends—it was not by chance that the Constitution empowers Congress to "promote the progress of science and useful arts" —and as friends they would extirpate at least "a portion of vice from the world."

Rush was a physician with a scientist's curiosity concerning diseases of the mind and the Enlightenment philosopher's confidence that the world stood on the threshold of discoveries that would transform the existence of man. His theories of punishment were derived directly from his reflections on the nature of what he called the moral faculty, which he first discussed in a paper, "An Enquiry into the Influence of Physical Causes upon the Moral Faculty," delivered before the American Philosophical Society in 1786, and published by the society that same year. He defined the moral faculty as a power in the mind of distinguishing and choosing good and evil, virtue and vice, and he likened it to a lawgiver (in the sense that it performs the the office of a lawgiver); the conscience, another power of the mind, he likened to a judge. The moral faculty is innate but is affected by physical causes, and it was one task of science to understand the relationship—for example, to understand whether the physical causes acted upon the moral faculty through the medium of the senses, the passions, the memory, or the imagination. He denied that his doctrine implied the materiality of the soul or, even if it did, that the doctrine of the immortality of the soul depends on its being immaterial. The important thing was to understand the physical causes of the moral faculty's disorders. This had not yet been done, which explained why "so few attempts [had] been made, to lessen or remove [the disorders] by physical as well as [by] rational and moral remedies."[16] He then sketched briefly fifteen factors that have, or seemed to have a capacity to produce effects on the moral faculty; of these, diet, idleness, bodily pain, solitude, silence, and medicine were, as he understood them, of special concern to the criminal law reformer. Idleness is the parent of every vice, he says, and "labor of all kinds, favors and facilitates the practice of virtue"; and he cites the prison reformer, John Howard, in support of his conclusion that labor is the most benevolent of punishments because it is one of the most suitable means of reformation.[17] Bodily pain has the effect of rousing and directing the moral faculty, and again he cites Howard's prison observations. Solitude removes bodies disposed to vice from the disquieting effects of society and renders them reformable, especially when solitude is combined with reflection and "instruction from books." Connected with solitude is silence. As to medicine, not much is known, but "may not the earth contain in its bowels, or upon its surface, antidotes to our moral, as well as to natural diseases?"[18] The quest for such medicines would be the task of future generations of scientists of the mind or of the psyche; this theory of the mind's faculties would, "when combined with the idea that each faculty was represented by a separate area in the brain,"[19] give rise to phrenology, which was to flourish for a while during the nineteenth century and to have some effect on criminology. Rush is responsible, in America, for the role played by scientists in the cultivation of the moral faculty, which, he says, must not be the business only of "parents, schoolmasters and divines."[20] If the scientists apply to this task the same industry and ingenuity that has produced the "triumphs of medicine over diseases and death," it is highly probable, he says, that vice might be banished from the earth.

I am not so sanguine as to suppose, that it is possible for man to acquire so much perfection from science, religion, liberty and good government, as to cease to be mortal; but I am fully persuaded, that from the combined action of causes, which operate at once upon the reason, the moral faculty, the passions, the senses, the brain, the nerves, the blood and the heart, it is possible to produce such a change in the moral character of man, as shall raise him to a resemblance of angels—nay more, to the likeness of God himself.[21]

Rush's portrait appears today on the seal of the American Psychiatric Association.

The first prison established in Philadelphia in 1790 did not embody all these principles; most significantly, the prisoners in it who worked together were contaminated by association, while those who were isolated one from another did not work. Gustave de Beaumont and Alexis de Tocqueville, who came to America in 1831 to study the penitentiary system, drew the conclusion that up to this point it could not be said that America had a penitentiary system.

If it be asked why this name was given to the system of imprisonment which had been established, we would answer, that then as well as now, the abolition of the punishment of death was confounded in America, with the penitentiary system. People said—*instead of killing the guilty, our laws put them in prison; hence we have a penitentiary system.*

The conclusion was not correct. . . . the penitentiary system does not necessarily exist [until] the criminal whose life has been spared, be placed in a prison, whose discipline renders him better.[22]

These faults were remedied in 1821 by the building of the Cherry Hill penitentiary, also in Philadelphia, as well as by the Auburn system inaugurated by the state of New York several years earlier.

The characteristic features of both systems, originally and as they existed during the visit of these two famous Frenchmen, were work, religious instruction, and solitary confinement, the principle being that any communication among the prisoners would lead to further criminalization and thereby make repentance impossible. In Philadelphia's Cherry Hill penitentiary, this principle was applied without qualification, each prisoner living, working, and eating in a cell of his own, exercising in a small yard adjoining his cell, and being visited by prison officials and almost nobody else. The Auburn system adopted the principle of isolation but modified it by requiring the prisoners to leave their solitary cells during the day in order to perform useful labor in the common workshops, but it obliged them to observe a rule of absolute silence during the period outside the cells. The prisoners would continue to reflect (and repent) in their isolation from one another, and the silence rule, enforced by the whip, would prevent their mutual criminalization, while the work in common would spare them the worst consequences of absolute isolation: severe depression, demoralization, and, indeed, insanity. So they were daily marched from their cells, but in lockstep and with heads bowed.

What was said about repentance was not a sham. The men who administered these new establishments were selected with great care and with scrupulous attention to the principles on which the institutions were founded. Beaumont and Tocqueville report that they were impressed by the importance attached to the selection of administrative personnel. The consequence was the conspicuous absence of the "vulgar jailer type," scarcely distinguishable from those put under his supervision, and the conspicuous presence of persons distinguished by their religiosity and genuine concern for the regeneration of the prisoners. "Moral and religious instruction forms . . . the whole basis of the system."[23] At Cherry Hill this was done by providing each prisoner with a Bible which he was encouraged to read and reflect upon and by visitations by carefully selected supervisory personnel who served as ministers and counselors; at Auburn religious services were conducted, sermons were carefully conceived and delivered, and the meals were preceded by the saying of prayers.

What is particularly striking about this early penitentiary system is the absolute confidence exhibited by its founders and supporters, not in the details of its administration—as to those there could be disagreement and doubt—but in its principles, and not only in its principles but in the right of society to punish and through punishment reform. Lest this be seen as an observation too obvious to make, the reader is asked to compare the attitude of some penologists—and amateur penologists—of our own day, for example, Ramsey Clark, Tom Wicker, and Karl Menninger, to say nothing of Jessica Mitford.* Behind Cherry Hill and the Auburn system was an unquestioned conviction that the laws were just, that they must be obeyed, that criminals were malefactors or, quite simply, bad men, and that society, for its own good and for the good of the criminals, had every right as well as the duty to subject them to this treatment. The treatment itself was right because it derived from the discoveries of the new moral and physical sciences. Here is the

*See below, pp. 76–82.

judgment of Francis Lieber, the translator of Beaumont and Tocqueville's study and a man who has a claim to the title of America's first professional political scientist:

The progress of mankind from physical force to the substitution of moral power in the art and science of government in general, is but very slow, but in none of its branches has this progress, which alone affords the standard by which we can judge of the civil development of a society, been more retarded than in the organization and discipline of prisons, probably for the simple reason that those for whom the prisons are established, are at the mercy of society, and therefore no mutual effort at amelioration, or struggle of different parties, can take place. At length the beginning has been made, and it is a matter of pride to every American, that the new penitentiary system has been first established and successfully practiced in his country. That community which first conceived the idea of abandoning the principle of mere physical force even in respect to prisons, and of treating their inmates as redeemable beings, who are subject to the same principles of action with the rest of mankind, though impelled by vitiated appetites and perverted desires; that community, which after a variety of unsuccessful trials, would nevertheless not give up the principle, but persevered in this novel experiment, until success has crowned its perseverance, must occupy an elevated place in the scale of political or social civilization. The American penitentiary system must be regarded as a new victory of mind over matter—the great and constant task of man.[24]

Such was the spirit of that age, and it is no wonder that the good men who characterized it and who addressed themselves to the problem of crime and punishment were convinced that the death penalty, which appeared to them as a vestige of a benighted past, had no place in the world they were creating. If Beaumont and Tocqueville had their doubts, and if, as a result, they were of the opinion that the penitentiary was not likely to render the death penalty obsolete or unnecessary (indeed, they considered it to be, in certain cases, "indispensable to the support of social order"),[25] this could be attributed to the fact that they were not Americans and, even more to the point, were not simply modern men, or reformers. They acknowledged the advantages of the American penitentiary system, especially when compared with the typical European prison, but they did so skeptically or reservedly, maintaining a critical distance from the enthusiastic reformers they encountered. As to these, they said there were in America as well as in Europe "estimable men whose minds feed upon philosophical reveries, and whose extreme sensibility feels the want of some illusion."

These men, for whom philanthropy has become a matter of necessity, find in the penitentiary system a nourishment for this generous passion. Starting from abstractions which deviate more or less from reality, they consider man, however far advanced in crime, as still susceptible of being brought back to virtue. They think that the most infamous being may yet recover the sentiment of honor; and pursuing consistently this opinion, they hope for an epoch when all criminals may be radically reformed, the prisons be entirely empty, and justice find no crimes to punish.[26]

Such men especially saw the penitentiary as a means of effecting a radical reformation, or of accomplishing a "complete regeneration," among an appreciable number of its criminal inmates, and Beaumont and Tocqueville denied this even as a possibility. Some "habits of order" could be instilled, they said, and if the typical prisoner on leaving these institutions were not in truth a better man, he might at least be more obedient to the laws, "and that is all . . . society has a right to demand." If the only goal of the pentitentiary were "radical reformation," they concluded, then it would be better to abandon it—"not because the aim is not an admirable one, but because it is too rarely obtained."[27]

But their reservations were as nothing when compared with the judgment of the next famous European visitor, Charles Dickens. Dickens visited Philadelphia and the Cherry Hill penitentiary in 1842, about ten years after Beaumont and Tocqueville, and whatever his opinion of the Auburn system, what he saw at Cherry Hill, or what he said he saw, appalled him. This, he assured his readers, was not due to a man of letter's disdain for social reformers or because the was prejudiced against Americans or, in particular, Philadelphians. In fact, he liked the city itself, although the regularity of its plan and the straightness of its streets distressed him—he would have given the world "for a crooked street"—and, within limits, he admired its Quaker inhabitants. But, as I said, he was appalled by the penitentiary system they had created. The benevolent intentions of the men who had devised it and were its directors he generously conceded, but he doubted that they knew "what it is they are doing." And what he said they were doing was inflicting "an immense amount of torture and agony" on those confined within its walls, and this with no discernible benefit. His account is one to which the adjective chilling may truly be applied:

Standing at the central point, and looking down these dreary passages, the dull repose and quiet that prevails, is awful. Occasionally there is a drowsy sound from some lone weaver's shuttle, or shoemaker's last, but it is stifled by the thick walls and heavy dungeon-door, and only serves to make the general stillness more profound. Over the head and face of every prisoner who comes into this melancholy house, a black hood is drawn; and in this dark shroud, an emblem of the curtain dropped between him and the living world, he is led to the cell from which he never again comes forth, until his whole term of imprisonment has expired. He never hears of wife or children; home or friends; the life or death of any single creature. He sees the prison-officers, but with that exception, he never looks upon a human countenance, or hears a human voice. He is a man buried alive; to be dug out in the slow round of years; and in the meantime dead to everything but torturing anxieties and horrible despair.[28]

This wretched man or woman has a Bible, of course, and a slate and a pencil, and the tools with which he performs his "rehabilitating" labor, and water and a slop bucket, but his cell is closed off by two solid doors through which he passes only twice, upon the commencement and the termination of his sentence. There "he labours, sleeps and wakes, and counts the seasons as they change, and grows old."

There was a sailor who had been there upwards of eleven years, and who in a few month's time would be free. Eleven years of solitary confinement!

"I am very glad to hear your time is nearly out." What does he say? Nothing. Why does he stare at his hands, and pick the flesh upon his fingers, and raise his eyes for an instant, every now and then, to those bare walls which have seen his head turn grey? It is a way he has sometimes [Dickens is told by his guide].

Does he never look men in the face, and does he always pluck at those hands of his, as though he were bent on parting skin and bone? It is his humour: nothing more.[29]

To which Dickens adds on his own, it is also his humor to be a helpless, crushed, and broken man. Not only that but deaf, as Dickens pointed out to the incredulous officials who regularly saw the prisoners, who had never noticed the phenomenon, and who disbelieved it until Dickens had it confirmed by a demonstration. And why not deaf? One would expect all the senses to be dulled and the bodily functions to be impaired; Dickens saw enough to conclude that this was typically the case.[30]

And what about their reformation? Dickens found no evidence that anyone had in fact repented. One man—"a very dexterous thief"—declared that he blessed the day he had been confined and that he would never "commit another robbery as long as he lived"; but his manner led Dickens to call this "unmitigated hypocrisy." As Beaumont and Tocqueville had observed ten years earlier, the convict "has an interest in showing to the chaplain . . . profound repentance for his crime, and a lively desire to return to virtue," which is a phenomenon the parole boards of our day have remarked; and the chaplain or other penitentiary official has an ardent wish to achieve the reformation of the criminal, and "easily gives credence to it,"[31] which, in turn, is a phenomenon remarked by those who in our day observe probation officers at work. (The administrative lesson to be drawn from this is that the evaluation of a reform program cannot be left in the hands of its friends, or in the hands of those hired by its friends.)

Perhaps it was not inevitable that the "house of repentance" become the sort of institution it is today—that the Auburn of the early nineteenth century in New York become the Attica of the twentieth—but it was not reasonable to think that the typical prisoner could be led, by any system, to become a genuine penitent. Some surely, but to build a system for the many that is contrived to benefit only the few is politically irresponsible. That was the conclusion drawn by Beaumont and Tocqueville: "an institution is only political if it is founded on the interest of the mass; it loses its character if it only profits a small number."[32] And the penitentiary system profited—and still profits —only a small number. There are those who insist it profits nobody.

Benjamin Rush began with the scientist's confidence that every problem has its solution and every disease its cure. He said just that. Since crime was a disease, it remained only to find the "remedy or remedies" appropriate to each of its manifestations; this inevitably meant a search for the treatment appropriate to each criminal. Hence, "let no notice be taken, in the law, of the punishment that awaits any particular crime." To the contrary, punishments should always be varied in degree "according to the temper of criminals, or the progress of their reformation."[33] In the event, it was not Rush's treatment that was established in the penitentiaries. Criminals were locked in solitary cells, made to work, and importuned to repent. At the outset, at least, there was a genuine attempt to classify them according to their crimes to the end of providing them with individualized treatment. But the administrative problems and costs of such a program were immense. A system of discrete treatments would have to wait upon the development of psychiatry (and beyond that) and the growth of the economy that is expected to pay for them. In the circumstances of the nineteenth century, the only variation in "treatment" was in the length of time presumed to be required to cause prisoners to repent, and in the course of time the penitentiaries ceased altogether to speak of repentance.

As early as the 1850s official commissions began to report the failure of the penitentiary system. Its object was to make the prisoner a better member of society, but this it did not succeed in doing, and very early it ceased to try. E. C. Wines and Theodore Dwight reported to the New York legislature in 1867 that there was not a state prison in the entire country that made the reformation of convicts the one supreme object of its discipline.[34] To say nothing of other reasons for this failure, the typical convict was functionally illiterate and therefore unable to read the Bible with which he was provided.

As wardens looked more closely at the actual nature of the inmate population, they lost patience with the goals of reform; as they lessened their insistence on silence and separation, security became more of a problem. The result was that they gave still less attention to rehabilitation. In short order they were complacently administering a custodial operation.[35]

And custodial operations they remain to this day.

The early penitentiary officials were not wholly wrong to look upon criminal behavior as a manifestation of the sickness of the soul, and their remedy, religious instruction leading to repentance, was, in principle, appropriate to what they understood to be the "disease." (I am not here referring to the range of remedies that Rush might have thought to be appropriate cures of the disorders of the mind's moral faculty.) Yet they seemed never to have given sufficient thought to the problem. Even Rush, who made so careful an analysis of public punishments and their probable effects on sensibility—"the sentinel of our moral faculty"—and who went into such detail concerning the desired effect of the prison on the community of law-abiding citizens, failed altogether to provide a description of the mechanism by which the proposed treatment would effect the reformation of the prisoner. He proposed to inflict bodily pain, of a sort and to a degree and of a duration to be determined by

58

the as yet undiscovered "principles of sensation [and] the sympathies which occur in the nervous system"; to this would be added "labour, watchfulness, solitude, and silence." Finally, as I mentioned earlier, and to "render these physical remedies more effectual," he proposed "regular instruction in the principles, and obligations of religion." Beyond this, all he said was that specific punishments must be prescribed for specific crimes; to discover them, "to find out the proper remedy or remedies for particular vices," was, he concluded, "the only difficulty." The difficulty was greater than he and, more to the point, the penitentiary officials, imagined.

To speak strictly, penitence requires one to acknowledge his transgression and to manifest the desire to be cleansed of it, as well as the willingness to pay the price required. It is similar to expiation insofar as the cleansing or the remission of the sin depends on the willingness of God to be appeased and, therefore, to withhold his punishment, although expiation is the older phenomenon and is usually associated with more wrathful gods, gods who demand payment rather than permit it. It is likely that such a god will be appeased only by a severe punishment inflicted on the guilty person or a member of his family. Thus, according to Homer, when Agamemnon killed the stag sacred to Artemis, she responded by spreading a pestilence among the Greek army and calming the winds, thereby keeping the Greek fleet in port, and she was appeased only by Agamemnon's agreement to sacrifice his daughter, Iphigenia. And in a somewhat different example, God said to Moses: "the land cannot be cleansed of the blood that is shed therein, but by the blood of him that shed it."[36] In Christian doctrine, however, God may be appeased by the transgressor's voluntary acceptance of punishment, the desire for the punishment being the condition of his being cleansed of his sin. Rather than insisting on or prescribing the punishment, God insists on the penance, or the contrition combined with the desire to make amendments; and the punishment serves only the secondary purpose of allowing the transgressor to demonstrate that he is truly penitent. The political significance of this consists in the following: whereas God knows whether the transgressor is truly penitent, and knows it without the actual imposition of the punishment, a state's penal authorities, lacking the power to examine the human heart, will require a demonstration, and this can consist only in the voluntary acceptance of punishment. Stated otherwise, penitence requires the transgressor, the lawbreaker, to punish himself rather than for the state to inflict punishment on him. The state makes punishment available to him as a kind of welfare service; if he accepts it willingly, he demonstrates that he is penitent—and also demonstrates the success of the penitentiary system. If he does not, he demonstrates that he is not penitent and is not fit to be released. In the event, of course, it will appear that the state is inflicting the punishment on the offender, and in this way a penitential, or penitentiary, system is only too likely to resemble expiation, except that it is a wrathful state, rather than a god, that is being appeased. The French penologist Gabriel Tarde explained publicly prescribed penitence in this way: "The penalty has thus become simply an external and social manifestation of remorse, remorse reinforced at the same time as it is attested by the visible and traditional form intelligible to all, with which it clothes itself."[37] The relevance of what might otherwise appear to be a digression should become clear in Tarde's next sentence: "Unfortunately, the penalty understood in this manner only prevails in ages of belief; it is exceedingly rare in our present time prisons [1890] and there is no hope that it will ever flourish in them again."

Benjamin Rush was a good man and the Pennsylvania Quakers were good men, justly famous for their good works; but the age in which Pennsylvania and New York established the first penitentiary systems was not a pious age. It is therefore not wonderful (to use that word in its older sense) that the penitentiaries did not succeed in making many, or even more than a few, of their inmates penitent. America's gods promise material rewards for hard work and do not have the temerity to threaten to spread pestilence or demand sacrifices: Americans can overcome pestilences, inoculate against plagues, and cause their ships to sail without wind. All of which is to say that America, a country that began by subordinating religion and adopting a policy of indifference as to how or even whether its citizens worship,[38] has not provided a setting congenial to repentance. Piety has not characterized American lives outside prison, and it was unreasonable to expect it to characterize the prisoners' lives inside. Moreover, as the First Amendment is now being interpreted, a serious penitential program under state or federal auspices, involving compulsory religious instruction, prayers, and whatever else is prescribed by those who are serious about the paying of penance, would run into probably insurmountable constitutional difficulties. Indeed, some reflection on what that amendment signifies ought to have discouraged the founders of the "penitentiaries."

The legacy we acquired from Benjamin Rush and the other early reformers is, however, not so much Attica as it is the designation of the Atticas of America as "correctional" institutions—along with the whole correctional apparatus: indeterminate sentences, staff psychiatrists, parole boards, probation officers, "diversion," and, of course, "rehabilitation." All this and more derives from that first sentence of his 1787 paper, namely, that the first purpose of punishment is "to reform the person who suffers it." A system whose first purpose is to reform those persons submitted to its care and cure is, inevitably, a system governed by experts in caring and curing—scientists, in fact—and they sometimes display a zeal that causes them to overstep the proper limits of what may properly be done to or for citizens of a liberal democracy. There was a period—happily, a brief period—when the correctional apparatus in some states included surgeons to perform the relatively simple sterilization operations required to prevent the transmission of "defective" genes from one generation to the next—the seat of the criminal tendency, so to speak, then being thought to be located in the testes or ovaries rather than in the soul or the mind. It was a mistake, and leading scientists denounced the program and its premise, but it had its advocates and some of its advocates occupied responsible political positions. The chief judge of Chicago's municipal court put the case for sexual sterilization in his 1923 presidential address to the eleventh annual meeting of the Eugenics Research Association: "Mendel's Law of Heredity" points the way toward the solution of the problem of mental deficiency, and mental deficiency is the principal cause of crimes of violence and "lies equally at the bottom of all intrinsic crimes."[39] Thus, the state may require vasectomies for males, which can be performed in any physician's office, and salpingectomies for females, which had better be done in hospitals since abdominal incisions are required to get at the fallopian tubes, which have to be cut or tied. Promoted by the American Eugenics Society, whose model sterilization law proposed compulsory sterilization for a wide variety of "socially inadequate classes," including the "criminalistic," some twenty-eight states adopted laws requiring the sterilization of inmates in state hospitals or, in some cases, convicted criminals in prisons.[40] The Supreme Court once upheld a Virginia law applied to mental defectives—"Three generations of imbeciles are enough," said Justice Oliver Wendell Holmes[41]—but Oklahoma's Habitual Criminal Sterilization Act was invalidated on equal protection grounds in 1942, and the effect was to write "finish" to this so-called "reform."[42] Nevertheless, the correctional institutions are still with us, and with them the correctional spirit.

Born in the early nineteenth century out of the most generous of sentiments but exaggerated expectations, the penitentiary still exists (as do scores of the penitentiaries built in that period), even though it has failed abysmally to fulfill its principal purpose. One recent critic refers to it as the most "disastrous survivor of the Enlightenment still gasping at a death-like life."[43] It is fashionable and may even be correct to call it a crime factory, although the men and women who end up in a maximum security prison like Attica are more than likely to be incorrigible criminals before they begin their sentences.[44] Still, the men of the Enlightenment were surely not wrong about the mutually contaminating effect of putting criminals together in a setting where each criminal is merely one among many and, at a minimum, is able to derive some comfort from the awareness of being at home, so to speak, in the one environment where he need not be ashamed, and, at a maximum, is further brutalized by those worse than himself who, because of their lack of scruples, will inevitably rule prison society (or any society that has not learned to subordinate ruthless strength to rules of justice). Whether Dickens would be more appalled by today's Attica and Auburn than he was by the Cherry Hill of his time is, however, by no means obvious, although today's reformers appear to be of the opinion that nothing could be worse than what we now have. Garry Wills probably speaks for them when he says the following:

> Prisons teach crime, instill it, inure men to it, trap men in it as a way of life. How could they do otherwise? The criminal is sequestered with other criminals, in conditions exacerbating the lowest drives of lonely and stranded men, men deprived of loved ones, of dignifying work, of pacifying amenities. . . . Smuggling, bullying, theft, drug traffic, homosexual menace are ways of life. Guards, themselves brutalized by the experience of prison, have to ignore most of the crimes inflicted on inmates, even when they do not connive at them, or incite them. Breaking up smuggling, extortion, and sex rings is dangerous and probably futile; better look the other way and live to collect one's pension. The less contact with all but the most exploitable inmates, the better.[45]

Even if we do not doubt the accuracy of this portrait as it is meant to apply to Attica and some others or quarrel with the judgment that they, and perhaps the typical penitentiary today,[46] like the Cherry Hill of Dickens' day, are inhuman places, it must be pointed out that there is a difference between them and Cherry Hill: with the exception of such places as the Cummins Prison Farm of Arkansas, the inhumanity of the Atticas is caused by the inmates not the institutions. Both the guards and the inmates may be brutes, but, if so, the system is one in which the guards are brutalized by the prisoners, not the other way around. The typical prison may offer no dignifying work, but the typical prisoner did not engage in dignifying work on the outside; there may indeed be smuggling, bullying, theft, drug traffic, and homosexual menace, but, except for the last, probably not much more than the typical prisoner was accustomed to before he became a prisoner. After all, the maximum security prison is the end of the punishment line, not the beginning, and to reach it the typical prisoner will have first been subjected to the milder punishments meted out by the criminal justice system. For example, 50 percent of all offenders are granted probation. As for the absence of "pacifying amenities," that all depends on what is meant, sports and books or heterosexual assignations. If Wills means the latter, he is right: the prisons do not provide them—at least, they do not as a policy provide them.

To take issue with the prison's critics is not to deny that the prisons are terrible places or to suggest that it is fruitless to hope that something can be done to improve them, and even the best of them. But what? The worst can be made to resemble the best, but then what? Even Garry Wills can only say that we must "do something, whatever we can." John Bartlow Martin said more than twenty years ago that the prisons should be abolished,[47] a cause more recently taken up by Jessica Mitford, who says either they should be abolished completely or retained as places for "as few as possible," which she reckons to be all but 75, 80, or 90 percent of the present prison population, who "could be freed tomorrow without

64

danger to the community or increase in the rate of crime."[48] (If this is so—and it is not so—it is somewhat surprising that she does not also advocate the abolition of the police, or all but 75, 80, or 90 percent of them.) In a recent study, William G. Nagel agrees that prisons ought to be abolished, but recognizes that something must take their place: "The prison, after all, is a substitute for capital and corporal punishment."[49] Rather than return to them, he proposes a variety of substitutes for the substitute, essentially an emphasis on rehabilitative programs. Ramsey Clark, attorney general of the United States under Lyndon Johnson and a prototype of the modern reformer, says that rehabilitation "must be the goal of modern corrections," and he promises that if it is, if every other aspect of the criminal justice system is subordinated to it, recidivism can be reduced to half of what it now is; not only that, we can *"prevent nearly all of the crime now suffered in America—if we care."*[50] But Garry Wills says rehabilitation is "the last grisly excuse" put forward by the advocates of the prison system; and Governor Jerry Brown of California said recently that we face a real problem with prisons: "They don't rehabilitate, they don't deter, they don't punish, and they don't protect."[51] As we shall see, he is mostly wrong: they do deter, they do protect, and, unless Wills, Wicker, Mitford, *et alia* are wholly mistaken in their observations, they do punish. He is right, however, when he says they do not rehabilitate. The failure of the nineteenth-century penitentiary system finds its parallel in the failure, or failures, of the twentieth-century rehabilitation programs, in America as well as elsewhere.

CONTEMPORARY REHABILITATION

Rehabilitation programs are many and various. They feature vocational training and academic education, group counseling, and individual psychotherapy; they involve juveniles and adults, men and women; they begin before incarceration among probationers and after incarceration among parolees; they take place inside the prisons and outside in the community, in a "milieu" that is carefully "supportive" or in one that is deliberately nonsupportive; they impose a close supervision or allow considerable freedom; they have been instituted in the United States, under both federal and state auspices, and in such other countries as Canada, Britain, New Zealand, Denmark, and Sweden. Thus, when Ramsey Clark says we can solve the crime problem *"if we care,"* and thereby suggests that criminologists and penologists have not yet cared, he is being grossly unfair to the thousands of skilled and devoted men and women who have designed and administered these programs and to the larger number of legislators who have voted the funds to support them. The problem is not that no one other than Ramsey Clark cares; the problem is that nothing works.

Most of these programs have been designed so as to permit them to be evaluated, which is to say, to determine whether they do work. For example, in one of the most celebrated of them, the California Youth Authority Community Treatment Project, youthful offenders are randomly assigned either to a control group that is incarcerated and in time released to the customary supervision or to an experimental group whose members are put immediately on probation and, according to an assessment of what is required in individual cases, assigned to foster homes, group therapy, or a program of individual psychotherapy. All those in the experimental group receive special counseling and tutoring and are observed by officers working with small case loads (one officer per 9.5 offenders, compared with one per 55 in the control group). The success of the program is then evaluated by comparing the rates of favorable and unfavorable discharges of the two groups. The more typical method of evaluation is to compare the recidivism rates of the control group and the group subjected to rehabilitative treatment; thus, a recent Canadian study compared the rate at which Ontario offenders returned to crime either after serving their full prison sentences or after being paroled from prison to a special rehabilitation program. Still other programs are evaluated by judging adjustment to prison life, vocational success, or, to mention one more criterion, adjustment to the general community, none of which is easy to measure. Indeed, even the recidivism rate is not a very precise measure, since in one study it may involve minor parole violations and, in another, actual arrests for the commission of crimes. At any rate, hundreds of programs have been instituted and evaluated in one way or another, and the resulting evaluative studies have recently been subjected to a scrupulous review by Robert Martinson, an American criminologist.

He and his colleagues were commissioned by the state of New York to "undertake a comprehensive survey of what was known about rehabilitation," with the view to assisting the state to replace its essentially custodial system of corrections with a program of rehabilitation that would work. Martinson searched the literature for all reports in the English language on "attempts at rehabilitation that had been made in our correction systems and those of other countries from 1945 through 1967." From the much larger number of these he selected 231 studies that were sufficiently clear and rigorous in their methodology to permit analysis and evaluation. What he had to report to New York is that nothing works: "these data, involving over two hundred studies and hundreds of thousands of individuals as they do, are the best available and give us very little reason to hope that we have in fact found a sure way of reducing recidivism through rehabilitation."[52] This does not mean no criminals are ever rehabilitated—of course there are such cases —but that we have yet to find a program that will rehabilitate significant numbers of criminals. Martinson concedes that some treatment programs may be working "to some extent," but adds that we do not know it because the available research is incapable of finding them; and he concedes that some successful program may in the future be devised—although he doubts it. Of course, he uncovered many programs that are said by their supporters to be successful but upon independent evaluation are found not to be so. For example, the success claimed for the California Youth Authority Community Treatment Project was found to be the result of the tendency of the probation officers to discriminate in favor of the experimental group and against the control group. In the case of the latter, parole was revoked for less serious offenses; in the case of the former, its members "continued to commit offenses" but they were, nevertheless, "permitted to remain on probation." In fact, "the experimentals were actually committing more offenses than their controls."[53] What is involved here is the phenomenon observed by Beaumont and Tocqueville 150 years ago: the parole officer, like the Cherry Hill chaplain, has an ardent wish to achieve the reformation (or, nowadays, the "rehabilitation") of the criminal and "easily gives credence to it."[54] The same phenomenon can manifest itself in the tendency of administrators to select for the rehabilitative program those offenders who are better risks, or are conceived to be more rehabilitative. This tendency accounted for the success claimed for the Ontario parole program.[55]

What is clear from all this, and clear to an increasing number of criminologists and penologists, is that we do not know how to rehabilitate criminals any more than the men of the early nineteenth century knew how to cause them to repent. Even Ramsey Clark now admits this.[56] There continue to be reformers who look upon crime as a disease, but there is no agreement on what is diseased and must therefore be treated and cured. Martinson reports on a Danish behavior modification program that was almost completely successful—it involved the castration of sex offenders, as the result of which their recidivism rate fell off to 3.5 percent, but not to zero (as Martinson comments, where there's a will there's apparently some sort of a way)—but the appropriate treatment for armed robbery or assault, to say nothing of grand larceny or conspiracy to obstruct justice, is not so readily identified. Where would the surgeon begin? What drug would the pharmacologist prescribe? What part of the body or what aspect of the psyche would be treated? These are intended to be simple questions for which, I think, there are no simple answers; yet there is a school of psychiatry that claims to possess the answers. More than a quarter of a century ago, Benjamin Karpman, then on the staff of St. Elizabeth's Hospital in Washington, D.C., said flatly that "criminality is without exception symptomatic of abnormal mental states and is an expression of them."[57] This being so, or said to be so, the conclusion is obvious and Karpman states it in a radical form:

. . . imprisonment and punishment do not present themselves as the proper methods of dealing with criminals. We have to treat them physically as sick people, which in every respect they are. It is no more reasonable to punish these individuals for behavior over which they have no control than it is to punish an individual for breathing through his mouth because of enlarged adenoids. . . . In the future, it is the hope of the more progressive elements in psychopathology and criminology that the guard and the jailer will be replaced by the nurse, and the judge by the psychiatrist, whose sole attempt will be to treat and cure the individual instead of merely to punish him.[58]

There is absolutely *no* evidence to support these expectations, largely because, except in the case of organic diseases of the brain which can indeed lead to abnormalities of behavior, there is no scientific basis for the use of the term mental illness.[59] "Hence," as Thomas Szasz says, "it is idle to ask whether our contemporary psychiatric practices are 'therapeutically' effective—when there is no disease for them to 'cure.' "[60] Again, there is no doubt that organic psychoses have known physiological causes; the problem arises with the much larger category of what are called functional psychoses. Karpman makes his case with examples of paranoid dementia praecox, hebephrenia, manic depression, and senile dementia, and to the layman it would appear to be a persuasive case. For example, it would appear to be more reasonable to attribute repeated sexual attacks on small children to what he calls senile dementia than to an uncomplicated, straightforward desire for a "meaningful sexual relationship," as we say today. Then one comes to realize that the term senile dementia is no more specific in its vernacular than the term "meaningful" is in its. There is now an enormous body of professional literature showing how unreliable are psychiatric evaluations (and predictions); what has provoked an interest in this literature is the prevalent practice of turning the question of mental institution commitments over to the exclusive determination of psychiatrists, but the findings are obviously relevant to the treatment of prisoners in correctional institutions. The literature has recently been reviewed by Bruce Ennis and Thomas Litwack (the one a lawyer and the other a psychiatrist), who demonstrate that both the diagnoses and the predictions made by psychiatrists are unreliable and likely to be invalid. Specifically, with regard to schizophrenia, affective psychoses, and paranoid states, each falling in the general category of functional psychoses, the chances of a second psychiatrist agreeing with the diagnosis of a first are barely better than 50–50, and sometimes no better than 40 percent. In other words, the experts cannot agree on what is allegedly wrong with a patient. Moreover, when a diagnosis takes the form of a prediction, which provides an opportunity to draw a conclusion as to its validity, the studies show it is likely to be wrong. (Predictions of dangerousness—made to determine whether a person may be released from an institution—are " 'incredibly inaccurate.' ") As to mental illness, Ennis and Litwack conclude that there "is no reason to believe that psychiatrists can determine who is 'mentally ill' or predict who requires involuntary care and treatment any more reliably and accurately than they can make other diagnoses and predictions."[61] The same studies were reviewed independently by Harvard law professor Alan M. Dershowitz and a team of assistants, and, finding the same answers, he concluded that "no legal rule should ever be phrased in medical terms [and] no legal decision should ever be turned over to the psychiatrist."[62] Unfortunately, as Ennis and Litwack point out, judges and legislators are not aware of these things,[63] which could explain Canada's recent decision to inaugurate a multimillion-dollar program of psychiatric services in correctional institutions (at a "per patient" cost double the "per inmate" cost, not counting the cost of the physical facilities), except that the Solicitor General Allmand—the same reformer who, regardless of public opinion, was determined to abolish capital punishment—was not in fact unaware of the studies mentioned here.[64] He preferred to listen to the psychiatrists who wrote the report, and they, like Karpman a quarter century earlier, insist that crime is, to a greater or lesser extent, a disease amenable to their treatment, their "healing" arts. One of Karpman's examples was kleptomania, and in one sentence he said enough to destroy his case. "In kleptomaniacs," he said, "we have individuals who steal, but their stealing has a number of important differences from ordinary theft."[65] Yes, indeed; and the criminal law is—and solicitors general and others in charge of the administration of the criminal law ought to be—primarily concerned with *ordinary* theft, of which there is an enormous quantity; and if psychiatry is to be of significant assistance to the law enforcement and correctional officials, it will have to explain the etiology not merely of organic psychoses, or even a "neurosis" like kleptomania, but of ordinary shoplifting, burglary, bank robbery, and the like (and, of course, come forward with the appropriate treatment). Until that time comes, there is every reason to accept Willie Sutton's simple explanation of why he robbed banks: "Because that's where the money is."

To the extent that rehabilitation programs do not involve psychiatric treatment or vocational training, they aim at "resocialization" or "adjustment" or the overcoming of "maladjustment"; and the reference group to which the convicted criminal is asked to adjust or with respect to which he is said to be badly adjusted is the general population which (for some reason) continues to be law-abiding. The difficulty in effecting a "cure" of the condition designated maladjustment can be glimpsed in the extent to which that general population is moved by the same desires as the criminals, principally the desire for material gain. The difference between them consists merely in the ways they go about achieving this: the one honestly and the other dishonestly. We need not decide whether the economists are *wholly* correct when they suggest that persons become criminals because, on the basis of a calculation of benefits and costs, the expected utility of crime exceeds that of honest business enterprise; many persons do become criminals and, in many cases, "not because their basic motivation differs from that of other persons."[66] Nor is it necessary to accept Freud's account of the development of the superego or conscience, which he depicts as the internalization of the dread of being discovered in criminal or sinful acts and giving rise to a sense of guilt.[67] Whatever the mechanism, the law-abiding person is likely to be deterred from committing crimes by the fear of punishment and by the lessons he has been taught: that it is wrong to kill and steal and bear false witness and covet a neighbor's house, wife, manservant, maidservant, and ox—or, in our day, his credit card. Whether or not he has been taught these salutary lessons, the criminal obviously has not been persuaded of the necessity to obey them. Edwin H. Sutherland and Donald R. Cressey, in what is probably the most highly respected criminology textbook, appear both to recognize the problem and to minimize the difficulties in overcoming it when they say that a greater effort should be made to socialize the criminal. They demonstrate no awareness of the harsh measures that cohesive groups have traditionally relied on: corporal punishment, "scarlet letters," and ostracism come to mind. They simply say that we ought "to develop an attitude of appreciation of ['group'] values." This, they say, would be "much more efficient" than relying on the threat of punishment.[68] No doubt; and, as Madison said in the 51st *Federalist,* if men were angels, government itself would be unnecessary. But today especially, when so little opprobrium is attached to criminal activities and when the overwhelming majority of crimes—indeed, when *almost all* crimes*—go unpunished, the criminal is likely to compare himself not with the law-abiding group but with the other criminals, who, even in the unlikely event of being apprehended, are able to escape punishment; and that comparison is likely to persuade him that his trouble consists not in his maladjustment but in the bad luck or stupidity that led to his being caught and imprisoned. At any rate, there is no evidence that the *typical* prisoner is sick with any disease that can be cured by social worker, sociologist, or psychiatrist; the theory that he is sick "overlooks—indeed, denies —both the normality of crime in society and the personal normality of a very large proportion of offenders."[69]

Recognition of the failure of reform, or of the utter inadequacy of what is called the "rehabilitative model" of penology, is the most striking aspect of contemporary criminology, and not merely in America. Misgivings that only a few years ago had to be expressed privately are now stated openly at meetings, seminars, workshops, and wherever crime and punishment are discussed by experts. It is no longer necessary in these circles to apologize for them. The point has been reached where even the Pennsylvania Quakers have begun to criticize their forebears for initiating the American penal reform movement. A recent report prepared for and published under the auspices

*See below, pp. 106–10.

of the American Friends Service Committee speaks of the "horror that is the American prison system [that] grew out of an eighteenth-century reform by Pennsylvania Quakers and others against the cruelty and futility of capital and corporal punishment."[70] This 200-year-old experiment, they say, has failed. Perhaps the best evidence of this new recognition of the failure of the rehabilitative model is to be found in the recent writings of Norval Morris, whose credentials as a leading criminologist will not be challenged by anyone. No criminal, he says emphatically, should ever be incarcerated for the purpose of treating him. The advocates of treatment have been led into serious error by their assumption that criminality is a disease in the same way that pneumonia is a disease; the analogy with physical medicine, he says, is false, and has for too long a time been allowed to dominate penology. Prisons should rehabilitate if they can; they should make rehabilitative facilities available to those prisoners who voluntarily submit themselves for treatment; but the purpose of punishment or imprisonment is not to reform offenders. The purpose is "properly retributive, deterrent, and incapacitative."[71] That it is now possible to speak of the propriety of retribution or subtitle an article in a highly respected journal, "Toward a Punitive Philosophy," or for another highly sophisticated group of professionals to write that "certain things are simply wrong and ought to be punished,"[72] is an index of this change that has occurred in our time.

CONCLUSION: BLAMING CRIME ON SOCIETY

The penal reform movement began in the United States when Benjamin Rush, moved by compassion and a faith in science, said that the first purpose of punishment was reform of the criminal. Since the death penalty was the punishment least calculated to achieve that end, it was to be replaced by the penitentiaries where criminals would be caused to repent and to learn to live new lives. In the course of time, the agents of this reformation changed from priests to general medical practitioners to social workers and psychiatrists, during which repentance gave way to rehabilitation, adjustment, and cure.

In his characterization of the struggle over the death penalty since Beccaria's time, Thorsten Sellin, as I indicated earlier, spoke of the contending forces as the ancient and deeply rooted beliefs in retribution, atonement, or vengeance on the one hand, and, on the other, beliefs in the "personal value and dignity of the common man."[73] It is not by chance, however, that the reform penology has profoundly *un*democratic consequences. Not only does it subject prisoners to courses of treatment against their will—a fact that has caused it to be criticized by prisoners and criminologists alike—but it substitutes rule by the few for rule by the people. Whether a particular mode of punishment or treatment will effect the reform of the criminal is an issue on which the public may or may not have opinions, but it is not an issue in whose resolution the public's opinion should be given any weight, even in a democracy. It is not a question of justice but of medicine and, as such, should be turned over to the experts in medicine, the psychiatrists, or whatever. Whether a particular criminal is in fact reformed is, of course, a question of fact, and should be answered by those who are alone qualified to answer it. They will determine when a criminal is cured, and, therefore, they will determine the length of sentence. Hence, the public's notion of justice that is embodied in every schedule of punishment must be superseded by indeterminate sentences, and, in penology, democracy must be superseded by what might be called psychotocracy. The belief in the "personal value and dignity of the common man" does not include a belief in his capacity to decide questions of punishment. Common men serve on juries and mete out death sentences; uncommon men serve on the Supreme Court and set aside those sentences, accusing juries of being arbitrary, capricious, bigoted, and cruel. Common men continue to be moved by the concern for the fitness that we call justice and that manifests itself in the rule that people should get what they deserve; our uncommon reformers insist that the issue is not one of justice but of medicine.

Having said this, I must immediately qualify it: there is a school of reformers that is very much concerned with what they understand to be justice. It is precisely their concern for justice that prevents them from following the trend in criminology away from the rehabilitative model and toward the punitive model. They agree that reform and rehabilitation have failed; what sets them apart from Norval Morris, for example, is their insistence that punishment is unjust. And what sets them apart from the earlier reformers is their opinion that society is unjust and, because it is unjust, has no right either to punish or to treat criminals. In their view, criminology has been at fault because it looked for the causes of crime in the soul or body of the criminal, whereas they are actually to be found in society or in the "conditions." It follows that it is the "rotten" society or the "system" that must be reformed, not those whom it labels criminals.

Thus, as the American Friends Service Committee sees it, most crimes are committed by the "agencies of government," just as most murders have been committed by governments.[74] Thus, too, as Tom Wicker sees it, Rockefeller was the cause of the Attica prison uprising, not Nelson Rockefeller the governor of New York, but the "other Rockefeller—all the Rockefellers of the world, the great owners and proprietors and investors and profit-makers." They had shaped the "society that had produced Attica."[75] It is the system that is "crime-breeding," insofar as anyone may be denominated a criminal or anything a crime. In fact, psychiatrist Karl Menninger suggests that the only crime in our midst is the one committed by those persons whom society perversely designates law-abiding:

And there is one crime we all keep committing, over and over. I accuse the reader of this—and myself, too—and all the nonreaders. We commit the crime of damning some of our fellow citizens with the label "criminal." And having done this, we force them through an experience that is soul-searing and dehumanizing. In this way we exculpate ourselves from the guilt *we* feel and tell ourselves that we do it to "correct" the "criminal" and make us all safer from crime. We commit this crime every day that we retain our present stupid, futile, abominable practices against detected offenders.[76]

We do this, he says, because we need crime: "The inescapable conclusion is that society secretly *wants* crime, *needs* crime, and gains definite satisfactions from the present mishandling of it!" We need it to "enjoy vicariously." We need criminals "to identify ourselves with"; they "represent our alter egos—our 'bad' selves." Criminals do for us the "illegal things we *wish* to do and, like scapegoats of old, they bear the burdens of our displaced guilt and punishment."[77] Them we can punish, he says; on them we can wreak our vengeance.[78]

It should be obvious that these are not the strictures of a Communist casting blame on the capitalist mode of production; this is the nonpartisan voice of what calls itself science. Menninger, recent winner of the Roscoe Pound Award for his outstanding work in "the field of criminal justice,"[79] looks at the crime problem "from the standpoint of one whose life has been spent in scientific work." He claims, and not unreasonably one would have thought, that the scientific perspective is superior to "commonsense" when it comes to understanding the causes of crime and the disposition or handling of so-called criminals. The common man's common sense says catch "criminals and lock them up; if they hit you, hit them back."[80] And what does his science say? Do away with punishment, of course, and, to the extent necessary, replace it with a system of penalties. To wit:

If a burglar takes my property, I would like to have it returned or paid for by him if possible, and the state ought to be reimbursed for its costs, too. This could be forcibly required to come from the burglar. This would be equitable; it would be just, and it would not be "punitive."[81]

That is, if the burglar is caught (but the chances of his being caught are statistically remote), do not punish him; "penalize" him by requiring him to return what he has stolen. "Scientific studies have shown that most punishment does not accomplish any of the purposes by which it is justified, but neither the law nor the public cares anything about that. The real justification for punishment is none of these rational 'purposes,' but an irrational zeal for inflicting pain upon one who has inflicted pain (or harm or loss)."[82] Our crime problem will not be solved until we reform ourselves, Menninger says time and again, and learn to love those we obdurately and mistakenly label criminals. "Love against Hate," is the revealing title of one chapter, in a book entitled *The Crime of Punishment.* The reform of the law of punishments can only be accomplished by abolishing punishment. Friedrich Nietzsche (whose diagnosis may be accepted even though his cure must be rejected) had these reformers in mind when, a century ago, he wrote the following:

> There is a point in the history of society when it becomes so pathologically soft and tender that among other things it sides even with those who harm it, criminals, and does this quite seriously and honestly. Punishing somehow seems unfair to it, and it is certain that imagining "punishment" and "being supposed to punish" hurts it, arouses fear in it. "Is it not enough to render him *undangerous?* Why still punish? Punishing itself is terrible."[83]

Benjamin Rush did not hate criminals, but neither did he love them or ask that they be loved. On the contrary, he disliked public executions because the sight of condemned men meeting their fate with fortitude was likely to cause them to be admired —and criminals were not to be admired—and the sight of their suffering was calculated to arouse the public's sympathy for them—and criminals were not to enjoy public sympathy. Hence, they were to be incarcerated in remote places (like Attica) where their punishment and rumors or legends about their punishment would "diffuse terror thro' [the] community, and thereby prevent crime." But he made reforming the criminal the first purpose of this punishment, and the solicitude required to effect this reform is not far distant from the love we are now asked to display. And it is not by chance that Menninger's demand that we love criminals is balanced by his harsh strictures against the public that persists in hating criminals and demands that they be paid back for their evil deeds. Nor is it by chance that Menninger expresses no sympathy for the victims of the crimes. They belong to the society that causes crime and must be reformed.

Quaker Elizabeth Fry, the distinguished early-nineteenth-century English prison reformer, did not hate criminals, but she nevertheless insisted that prison reformers must maintain a dignified distance from them precisely because the reformers must provide an exemplary model for their emulation. She said it was not safe "in our intercourse with them to descend to familiarity—for there is a dignity in the Christian character which demands and will obtain respect." Our contemporary Quakers quote this passage and then denounce her advice as the sort of paternalism that has "infected" much penal reform.[84] The fault in our "correctional practice" has consisted in the attempt on the part of Elizabeth Fry and her successors to indoctrinate prisoners in "White Anglo-Saxon middle-class values."[85] This fault merely reflects the more basic fault in society's failure to encourage the creation of "morally autonomous" people.[86]

So say our present-day Quakers; and when even the Quakers begin to speak the idiom of the counterculture, it is surely time to forget about reforming criminals. However misguided were the reform efforts of the early Quakers, they at least possessed one quality that is a necessary condition of reform: the confidence that they were right and the criminals were wrong. Their descendants lack that confidence. They do not speak of "resocialization," "adjustment," or "maladjustment," because they hate the society and will not ask anyone to adjust to it.

The reform movement that Benjamin Rush began in the late eighteenth century can be said to have culminated in a dramatic scene in Attica's D-yard during what may have been the worst and what was surely the most publicized prison revolt in American history. Here the pathologically soft reformer, in the person of an editor of the country's most powerful newspaper, appeared on the scene as a "neutral" observer. Beset with guilt, he ignored the hostages being held by the convicts, denounced the society that causes crime and builds Atticas, sobbed, he said, as he listened to the "authentic" eloquence of convicts' speeches, and finally threw his arms around the convict who had called out his name, hugging him to his breast. " 'We gonna win, brother,' Wicker says. 'We gonna win.' The boy smiled and nodded and Wicker walked on, thinking he was *free at last free at last.* "[87]

Reformers, particularly those who are attached to the "rehabilitative ideal," are quick to blame the "system" for what the rest of us call crime, but, in fact, their responsibility for it cannot be ignored and should not be minimized. Criminal lawyers have pointed out, here in the words of Francis Allen, dean of the University of Michigan Law School, that "the concentration of interest on the nature and needs of the criminal has resulted in a remarkable absence of interest in the nature of crime,"[88] but that is only part of the story. It has also resulted in a remarkable lack of interest in the crimes that have been committed, contributing in turn to the remarkable sympathy for criminals manifested by criminologists, amateur and professional, as well as by some judges and politicians. Wicker embraces the criminal without knowing what crime he committed; Wicker has no interest in that. Camus devotes his remarkable rhetorical powers to put us in the criminal's place, to put our heads on the block, so to speak; but he ignores the criminal's victim. It is said to be a "butchery" to execute a convicted

murderer, but in weighing the case for and against capital punishment we are supposed to ignore the butchery of the crimes
these murderers commit. That is supposed to be irrelevant. In
the recent Canadian debate on the bill to abolish capital punishment, the prime minister, Pierre Trudeau, went so far as to say
to the opponents of the bill that if they succeeded, "some people are going to be hanged," and that the opponents of the bill
could not "escape their personal share of responsibility for the
hangings which will take place if the bill is defeated."[89] Think
of the criminals, of the "people" who would die if the bill failed
of passage, and do not think of the people who have already
died at the hands of the murderers. No one replied: "Of course.
That is the whole point of our opposition to this bill, that
murderers ought to die." The bill passed by a margin of 133–
125.

In prescribing punishments, it is natural to look at the crime;
in prescribing treatment, one looks at the patient (the criminal)
and ignores his crime. The sight of crime and the criminal
arouses anger, but the sight of someone suffering with a disease
arouses compassion for him. Anger with crime is naturally combined with compassion for the victims of crimes, and this is as
it should be: persons who are angry with crime and criminals
and feel sorry for the victims of crime are likely to be law-
abiding citizens. And the legal system that allows them to express that anger (or expresses it in their name) and to express
that compassion is a legal system that is doing a proper job; it
is teaching the lesson that a society of law must somehow teach.
It is acting as a moral legal system when it blames immorality,
or crime, and when it praises morality, or obedience to law. The
system favored by the modern reformers is the opposite of a
moral legal system. Like the unsophisticated citizen, our modern reformers are both compassionate and angry men, but their
compassion is felt for the criminal and their anger is directed at
society. Society is said to be responsible for the criminal's disease.

The effect of the "rehabilitative ideal" on crime and the criminal justice system has been pernicious. It has, as I shall argue in the next chapter, made it more difficult to apprehend, convict, and punish criminals, and, therefore, it has contributed to the increase in the number of crimes, including murders, being committed.

CHAPTER III

The Deterrence Question
and
the Deterrence Problem

THE PROGRESS OF CIVILIZATION, we are told and have reason to believe, has resulted in a vast change alike in the theory and in the method of punishment, and the changes in the method are related to the changes in the theory. In primitive societies, the right to punish was retained by the private party (or his family) that suffered the wrong, and punishment was likely to be vindictive or retributive, imposed in order to satisfy the desire to be avenged.[1] The legalizing or "socializing" of punishment did not immediately lead to the civilizing of the method of punishment, which continued to be characterized by vindictiveness. Offenders were burned at the stake, hanged and quartered, disemboweled, or otherwise mutilated. A good deal of ingenuity was employed in devising painful punishments, and, if we are to judge by what was done, the purpose of premodern punishment was simply to cause pain. This is no longer the case. The purpose of modern punishment (to the extent that punishment is permitted) is, in principle, to instill fear. This change is the consequence of a change in the ends of civil society itself.

Criminal law reform began 200 years ago when Beccaria applied to crimes and punishments the liberal principles delineated by the philosophers of natural rights. These rights were possessed in the state of nature but they were not enjoyed there because the state of nature resembled too closely the state of war of every man against every man. To secure these rights, governments had to be instituted among men; to provide this security became the chief end of government, which is to say that peace, so conspicuously absent both in the state of nature and in the preliberal state, became the chief end of government. To achieve it required a new kind of civil society.

His experience convinced Hobbes, the first of the natural rights philosophers,[2] that peace was endangered most of all by the seditious doctrine (which he called "one of the *diseases* of a commonwealth") according to which every private man is judge of good and evil actions and of the justice and injustice of the laws. This doctrine, so pernicious in its consequences, was fostered most of all by the clergy—Hobbes's *"ghostly"* or *"spiritual"* authority—and so long as the power of the clergy remained intact, men would continue to offer the sovereign only a conditional obedience because they would fear eternal damnation more than the sovereign's laws. This subjected the commonwealth to the continual and "great danger of civil war and dissolution."[3] Peace, then, required that men be rid of this unreasonable fear of "the power of spirits invisible";[4] peace required enlightenment. The enlightened sovereign would subordinate the spiritual authority and, in Beccaria's words, "see to it that men fear the laws and fear nothing else."[5] The true measure of crimes was not in their intrinsic character but in the "harm done to society." This palpable truth, so long obscured by the clergy working on "the timid credulity of men," would, as a consequence of the "present enlightenment,"[6] soon be made evident to everyone. The fear of God would be super-seded by the fear of the sovereign or the laws.

Liberated from the rule of the clergy, men would be less inclined to make war on the secular authority; unfortunately, they would also be more inclined to pursue their self-interest exclusively, because they would no longer be taught that it is wrong to do so. At least, the old moral teachings would lose the authority they formerly possessed. At this juncture, it would become essential to demonstrate to men that it is dangerous to pursue their interests in a manner forbidden by the laws. To convince them of this danger would be the function of punish-ment. With Hobbes, and even more explicitly with Beccaria, the purpose of punishment became the solid and prosaic necessity to make men obey the laws. Its purpose was not, said Hobbes, to exact revenge, but to instill "terror," to the end of correcting the offender and the others who might learn from the example.[7] Revenge looks to the past and is justified on the principle that the person on whom it is to be taken has done something for which he "deserves" to be punished. Strictly speaking, no one in the new liberal state would be punished because he had done something that merits punishment; he would be punished only to prevent future criminal behavior, either on his part or on the part of others. The penal law of the liberal state would, in a sense, have only prospective vision, looking not to the past but to the future. In short, the purpose of punishment would be to deter crimes and thereby ensure obedience to the laws. As Bec-caria put it, its purpose was "only to prevent the criminal from inflicting new injuries on . . . citizens and to deter others from similar acts."[8] Punishment deters crimes, it was assumed, be-cause it makes men afraid to commit them, and the laws depend on this fear. "What is the political intent of punishment?" he asked. "To instill fear in other men."[9]

Here, then, is the origin of the modern idea of deterrence. Here, in fact, is the origin of the idea of a civil society that would depend not on the word of God or the fear of God, but on the fear of punishment for its very existence. Unlike the system it was intended to replace, the liberal state would not depend on a moral education designed to teach men to love their neighbors as themselves; not only was such an education the cause of moral pretentions and, therefore, of civil disobedience and dissolution, but it did not in fact succeed in promoting concern for the well-being of others. It did not do so because, in Beccaria's words, it was opposed by a "force, similar to gravity, which impels us to seek our own well-being."[10] That force—self-interest or self-love—can be "restrained in its operation only to the extent that obstacles are set up against it," and the only obstacle that can be relied on is punishment. Punishments "prevent the bad effect without destroying the impelling cause, which is that sensibility [self-interest or self-love] inseparable from man." The liberal legislator, instead of using a church united to the state whose purpose is to teach men to be good (it was precisely that sort of thing from which its citizens were to be liberated), would emulate the "able architect whose function it is to check the destructive tendencies of gravity and to align correctly those that contribute to the strength of the building." Instead of attempting to suppress self-interest, the liberal legislator would build on it and rely on the fear of punishment to check or restrain its anti-social tendencies. As I said at the beginning of this chapter, the purpose of modern punishment, or, more precisely now, the modern purpose of punishment, would be to instill fear and thereby deter crime.

This liberal "scheme" had its critics, of course; Edmund Burke called it a "barbarous philosophy" according to which "laws are to be supported only by their own terrors, and by the concern which each individual may find in them from his own private speculations, or can spare to them from his own private interests."[11] He portrayed the essence of it in this vivid and singularly appropriate figure: "In the groves of *their* academy, at the end of every vista, you see nothing but the gallows." But in fact Beccaria was confident that the laws could be terrifying without resort to the gallows.

Throughout its long history as a legal penalty, capital punishment has been imposed because those in authority regarded it as the only penalty appropriate to or commensurate with the crime for which it was imposed or because they regarded it as the most awful penalty and had reason to believe (or simply believed) that most people so regarded it and would, therefore, seek to avoid it beyond all others. The abolitionists regard it as the most awful penalty ("an atavistic butchery")[12] and, when referring to the public's unwillingness to witness executions or a jury's reluctance to impose death sentences, suggest that most people are of the same opinion. But they nevertheless insist that, although it is feared beyond all other sanctions, the death penalty is not a more effective deterrent than imprisonment. Whether they are entitled to hold this opinion is the subject of the section that follows.

THE ARGUMENT AGAINST DETERRENCE

The murder rate almost doubled in the United States in the years 1960 through 1974, and the number of executions gradually declined until, in 1968, it reached zero; but it does not follow that these trends are causally connected. Common sense would suggest that they are somehow and to some extent related, but common sense is often mistaken and gives way to science, occasionally even to social science. Unfortunately, in this case it is not easy for social science to provide a reliable answer.

There are a number of reasons for this inability, the most obvious being the difficulty in identifying the effect of one among many factors that probably affect the murder rate. Just as we have reason to believe that a soybean plant, to choose a simple illustration, requires more than sunlight to grow to its optimum height, we suspect that the murder rate depends on factors in addition to the severity and kinds of punishments imposed on murderers; in fact, we suspect that many more (and more obscure) factors are involved than in the case of soybean culture. We might speculate that the number of murders by poison depends to some extent on the availability of lethal poisons—whether they may be obtained without prescription and whether the drugstores selling them are distributed throughout the area being studied—as well as on their price and the ease with which they can be administered. We might also speculate that the number of murders by shooting depends on the number of handguns in the community, on whether a license is required to purchase and carry them, and on their cost. It is also possible that the murder rate is sensitive to the amount of violence shown on television, as well as to the amount of poverty and unemployment, or that it depends on the efficiency of the police, the state of medical science, the proportion of the population in a particular age group, and so on. To isolate the effect of any one of these factors—say, the rate of executions —it is necessary to hold constant all the others, which sounds simple but is not. As I pointed out in the first chapter, Thorsten Sellin, the most representative and influential student of the deterrence question, attempted to solve this problem by studying the homicide rates in contiguous states, some with and some without the death penalty, on the assumption that these states "are as alike as possible in . . . character of population, social and economic conditions, etc." His conclusion was that the death penalty has no effect on the murder rate,[13] and most criminologists were convinced by his study, even though Sellin did not overcome all the difficulties involved in this kind of study.

In the first place, Sellin looked for correlations between the homicide rate and the legal status of the death penalty, rather than the number of executions actually carried out in the states where it was a legal punishment; but the number of executions is much more likely to have an effect on potential killers than the mere legal existence of the penalty. Then, although it may be true that contiguous states are similar with respect to the sociological factors that are thought to impinge on the homicide rate, it may also be untrue; and without thorough investigation, which he did not undertake, Sellin had no way of knowing whether the states he assumed to be equal in all other respects were, for one example, equally adept in apprehending and convicting those who committed murder. All of which is to say that this sort of simple cross-state comparison, even a cross-contiguous-state comparison, does not and cannot adequately "control" for the other factors.

This difficulty can be avoided by studying the murder rate within a state that has abolished the death penalty and then (most conveniently for the social science researcher) reimposed it. Unfortunately, most of the states that abolished the death penalty did so many years ago (Michigan was the first in 1846) when the statistics are either unavailable or especially unreliable. On the basis of the information that is available, however, Professor Sellin reached the conclusion reported above. But again there is an obvious difficulty: whereas a simple cross-state comparison cannot "control" for the factors that may differ from state to state, a simple cross-time comparison within one state cannot "control" for the factors that may differ from time to time.

Then there is the problem of distinguishing between incapacitation and deterrence. It is entirely possible that the death penalty prevents murders only because it prevents known murderers from committing additional murders and not because it "deters" potential murderers. The distinction is obviously of direct relevance to the deterrence issue, because known murderers can be incapacitated by imprisoning them (if we ignore the problem of the murders they commit in prison and the possibility that they might escape) as well as by executing them.

One other difficulty deserves mention. Whereas the plant scientist can assume that the height of a soybean plant may depend on the amount of sunlight it receives, his testing of this assumption is not complicated by the necessity to consider the possibility that the amount of sunlight may be affected by the height of his soybeans. The social scientist cannot ignore the equivalent assumption concerning executions and the murder rate. While executions may tend to produce a decline in the murder rate, it is entirely possible that both the number and rate of executions increase with the murder rate. The reason for this is that when the murder rate is high, or is perceived to be high, judges and juries may impose the death sentence on a larger proportion of convicted murderers than when it is low or is perceived to be low. Thus, the number of executions may be both cause and effect of the murder rate. One implication of this is that an increase in the number of executions "caused" by an increase in the murder rate may appear to be an increase in the murder rate "caused" by an increase in the number of executions. No simple technique can distinguish the two. Then, again, juries may be reluctant to convict under a statute that makes the death sentence mandatory for first-degree murder and, instead, bring in verdicts of guilty of manslaughter. This would give the appearance of a case where the threat of capital punishment "causes" a decline in the murder rate.

Despite these technical difficulties, there have been a number of studies of deterrence in addition to those conducted by Professor Sellin, and, until recently, there was uniformity and consistency in their findings. In the words of Norval Morris and Gordon Hawkins, the conclusion that emerges from these studies, "and from all the literature and research reports on the death penalty is, to the point of monotony: the existence or nonexistence of capital punishment is irrelevant to the murder, or attempted murder, rate." This, they say, "is as well established as any other proposition in social science."[14] Other researchers have denied this assertion and, in the course of doing so, have suggested that the criminologists were convinced by the studies because they wanted to be convinced.

It has been said that the studies on which they rely were undertaken under the assumption that punishment in general does not deter crime in general.[15] Hugo Adam Bedau, perhaps the best known of America's abolitionists, lent some substance to this charge when he conceded that some criminologists were skeptical of the death penalty's capacity to deter because they doubted the capacity of any punishment to deter "crimes of personal violence."[16] Such an opinion would appear to be extravagant (and Bedau does not share it), but it is held by reputable criminologists. As recently as 1967 Walter Reckless, in the fourth edition of his textbook, said flatly that punishment "does not . . . prevent crime in others or prevent relapse into crime [on the part of those who are punished]";[17] and even in 1974, a leading opponent of the death penalty, William J. Bowers, claimed that recent research "casts serious doubt on the deterrent efficacy of imprisonment."[18] Of course, such assertions have not gone unchallenged. Paul W. Tappan, the author of a leading textbook, characterized them as "dogmatic," "highly simplified," and the product of "loose thinking and naive criminological idealism."

As an argument for the abolition of the deterrent doctrine, it is often maintained that neither the threat nor application of penalties does prevent crimes. This position reflects the simplistic notion, too commonly prevailing in matters of social action, that nothing has been achieved merely because not everything is accomplished that we should like. It is sometimes said that high crime rates prove that sanctions do not deter or that penalties actually invite the crimes of men who seek punishment to dissolve their feelings of guilt. With tiresome frequency the illustration is cited of the pickpockets who actively plied their trade in the shadows of the gallows from which their fellow knaves were strung. These assertions have a superficial relevance but they do not dispose of the issue by any means.[19]

It has also been charged that the social science studies of the death penalty were undertaken solely "to disprove the deterrent value claimed for that punishment"[20] and, even more seriously, that criminologists became "advocates and spokesmen for the treatment interest and the treatment ideology, and did everything in their power to ridicule the very idea of deterrence."[21] All this may or may not be true; what is beyond question, I think, is that most studies of deterrence were undertaken by criminologists who were inveterate opponents of capital punishment, and their opposition, as the following examples are intended to show, may have influenced their work.

Canada's decision in 1967 to abolish capital punishment for a trial period of five years provided criminologists with a good opportunity to observe the consequences of this change in the penal law. Furthermore, in this case inquiry was facilitated by the availability of reliable statistics: Canada has a uniform national crime reporting system which, among other data, provides the researcher with accurate figures of the number of violent crimes committed each year, including criminal homicides and attempted murders. Working with these, Ezzat A. Fattah, in a study sponsored by the solicitor general of Canada, found that the "slight" increase in criminal homicide in Canada in recent years cannot be attributed to the suspension of capital punishment.[22] He arrived at this conclusion by comparing the increase in the criminal homicide rate with the increase in the rates of other violent crimes (for which there had been no change in punishments), and, among other things, found it to be "the *lowest* among all crimes of violence studied." Something other than the abolition of the death penalty had caused this increase, he concluded. The figures are presented in Table 1. The solicitor general relied on these findings to support his vigorous advocacy of complete and permanent abolition of the death penalty.

TABLE 1

Changes in Crimes of Violence, 1962–1970

			Canada			
	1970					
Offense	Number	Rate per 100,000 Population 7 Years and over	Percentage Change Over 1969		Percentage Change Over 1962	
			Number	Rate	Number	Rate
Criminal Homicide (Murder and Manslaughter)	425	2.3	+10.1	+9.5	+60.4	+35.3
Attempted Murder	260	1.4	+20.4	+16.7	+213.3	+180.0
Wounding and Assaults	78,979	424.4	+7.1	+4.8	+171.6	+125.1
Rape	1,079	5.8	+5.9	+3.6	+86.4	+52.6
Robbery	11,630	62.5	+16.0	+13.4	+134.9	+94.7

SOURCE: Ezzat A. Fattah, "The Canadian Experiment with Abolition of the Death Penalty," in William J. Bowers, *Executions in America* (Lexington, Mass.: Heath, 1974), p. 130.

Yet, even a cursory examination of Table 1 should make one pause. While the increase in the rate of criminal homicide is the lowest "among all crimes of violence studied," the increase in the rate of attempted murder is the highest of all the violent crime rates reported, a fact Fattah ignored. This increase may or may not be significant; before drawing conclusions one would have to know, for example, whether it represents an actual increase or merely an increase attributable to changes in prosecutorial practices: many of the offenses now designated "attempted murder" may have been prosecuted as aggravated

93

assaults in the past. Even the best of crime statistics are rendered unreliable to a degree by the discretion that police and prosecutors must exercise in the course of their work. It is even possible (but not probable) that an advance in medical treatment during this period, or in the speed with which it was made available, had the effect of saving lives that would have been lost in the past, thereby increasing the number of attempted murders while reducing (or subtracting from) the number of murders. Working with crime statistics is beset with difficulties.

Unfortunately, this is not the only place where Fattah was less than comprehensive in his reporting. The suspension of the death penalty in Canada did not extend to the crime of murdering policemen (and others, such as prison guards), and Fattah examined the number of these murders and claimed further support for his conclusion that the abolition of the death penalty did not cause an increase in the murder rate.

> If the increase in criminal homicide were due to the suspension of capital punishment, then the categories of murder for which this punishment has been retained should not show an increase. Since the murder of a policeman is still legally punishable by death, one would expect, if the increase in other types of homicide were due to the suspension of the death penalty, that this category would not be affected. Our data show that this is not true. The murder of policemen has been on the increase since the legal suspension of capital punishment in 1968 and despite the fact that it has been retained for this type of killing.[23]

This conclusion would be more acceptable were it not for the fact—and it is a fact well known to the public generally and to Fattah in particular—that the "last execution in Canada took place in 1962."[24] The potential murderers of policemen, like the potential murderers of everyone else, had good reason to know that even if apprehended and convicted they would not be executed: the latter may not be put to death and the death sentences imposed on the former will be (and all were) commuted to life imprisonment. In practice, then, there has been no difference in the punishments actually carried out, and Fattah's conclusion resting on the difference in the punishments that might have been carried out is not worth very much, to say the least. In effect, Canada has been without the death penalty since 1962 (and in 1976 abolished it by statute).

Another study, cited almost as frequently as Sellin's, is Karl Schuessler's 1952 time series analysis of execution and homicide data from various states. He, too, concluded "that the death penalty has little if anything to do with the relative occurrence of murder,"[25] but not all of his findings support this conclusion. He devised a test of deterrence that measured the relation between the risk of execution and the homicide rate in forty-one death-penalty states during the period 1937–49. What he found was "a slight tendency for the homicide rate to diminish as the probability of execution increases."[26] But the simple correlation coefficient between these two indices was a negative 0.26, and, in the circumstances, this figure was by no means insignificant.[27] Then, as a check on the consistency of this trend, he computed the ratio of the (average) execution rate to the (average) homicide rate for four groupings of these states. The results are presented in Table 2. In the text accompanying the table, he said this "shows that the homicide rate does not consistently fall as the risk of execution increases."[28] True enough, and I doubt that anyone would be so bold as to assert that the homicide rate would *consistently* fall as the risk of execution increases. But the table also shows that the group of states with the highest ratio of the average execution rate to the average homicide rate ($\frac{ER}{HR} = 0.25$) had the *lowest* homicide rate (2.0), as is to be expected—*if* executions deter homicide.

Let us look at one more example of a study that claims to show that the death penalty does not deter murder. William Bowers, outspoken opponent of capital punishment, did a study similar to Sellin's in which he compared the murder rates in nine sets of contiguous states in the eight years prior and subsequent to the moratorium on executions in the 1960s. He said he found "no evidence to suggest that the death

TABLE 2

Average Homicide and Execution Rates in Forty-one States Grouped According to Size of Homicide Rate

Quartile by homicide rate	Average homicide rate (HR)	Average execution rate (ER)	ER / HR
Highest	15.4	.32	.21
Upper middle	7.8	.14	.18
Lower middle	4.2	.08	.19
Lowest	2.0	.05	.25

SOURCE: Karl F. Schuessler, "The Deterrent Influence of the Death Penalty," *Annals of the American Academy of Political and Social Science* 284 (1952): 60.

penalty is a uniquely deterrent form of punishment."[29] The quality of this study is fairly indicated in this critical comment:

. . . the plain fact is that *none* of the states in eight of the nine groups had a single execution throughout this period. And in the ninth group, Bowers creates a dubious distinction between New York, classified as abolitionist, and New Jersey and Pennsylvania, classified as retentionist, although New York ceased all executions in 1963—the same year as New Jersey and one year after Pennsylvania. That such comparisons are used as a basis for inference about the deterrent effect of capital punishment taxes one's imagination.[30]

Bowers ends with some sharp words about the proponents of capital punishment and accuses them of relying on arguments that "depend on alleged faults in the existing research."[31] But enough has been said here to indicate that these allegations have some basis and that these various studies are not faultless. They surely do not justify the inferences drawn from them by their authors as well as by abolitionists outside the academic community. "Hanging is not a deterrent,"[32] we are told with some frequency; but such statements derive from partisan commitment not science.

THE ARGUMENT FOR DETERRENCE

Hugo Adam Bedau, much to his credit, was more modest in his assessment of what has been found by the various studies on deterrence. He said the proposition that the death penalty is a superior deterrent to life imprisonment has not been disproved, nor has it been confirmed. He nevertheless insisted it had been "disconfirmed" by the uniformity or consistency of the findings published.[33] His conclusion took the form of a challenge to the proponents of capital punishment:

> The death penalty is a sufficiently momentous matter and of sufficient controversy that the admittedly imperfect evidence assembled over the past generation by those friendly to abolition should now be countered by evidence tending to support the opposite [pro-capital punishment] position. It remains a somewhat sad curiosity that nothing of the sort has happened; no one has ever published research tending to show, however inconclusively, that the death penalty after all is a deterrent and a superior deterrent to "life" imprisonment. Among scholars at least, if not among legislators and other politicians, the perennial appeal to burden of proof really ought to give way to offering of proof by those interested enough to argue the issue.[34]

This was written in 1970. In the spring of 1975, the solicitor general of the United States, Robert H. Bork, in his *amicus* brief filed with the Supreme Court in *Fowler* v. *North Carolina*, a death-penalty murder case, referred to a new study that, he said, provided "important empirical support for the *a priori* logical belief that use of the death penalty decreases the number of murders."[35] The cited study, copies of which he had filed with each of the nine justices, was written by Isaac Ehrlich, a University of Chicago econometrician. In the published version of this study, Ehrlich concluded that "on the average the tradeoff between the execution of an offender and the lives of potential victims it might have saved was of the order of magnitude of 1 for 8 for the period 1933–67 in the United States,"[36] or, as this was reported in the press, "each execution may deter as many as eight murders."[37] Here, then, was the study Bedau had called for, but the response from the abolitionists was one of outrage. One of them immediately denounced it as "utter garbage."[38] Bedau himself charged the solicitor general with using the study as an attempt "to throw dust in our eyes," and then, choosing a figure of speech singularly inappropriate to his cause, announced that "the abolitionists are getting their hired guns out, too, to torpedo Ehrlich."[39] But Ehrlich was not a hired gun (he has said that he opposes capital punishment) and his study is not garbage.

Instead of comparing the murder rate and the legal status of the death penalty from state to state or over time within single states, Ehrlich employed multiple regression analysis, a technique that is frequently used by econometricians to investigate the possible relationship between one of a number of possible "causes," or independent variables, and a particular "effect," or dependent variable. He constructed a mathematical model of a "murder supply function" and treated its elements as his fellow econometricians treat inflation, the bank discount rate, or increases in the rate of the money supply. Just as they look to and gather economic data from the past to draw conclusions concerning the relative influence of a variety of factors on a described or measurable condition, and then offer advice as to how to achieve or avoid that condition in the future, he assumed it might be possible to gather past criminal and other statistics to draw conclusions concerning the factors that influence the crime rate, specifically the murder rate. (In an earlier study he purported to show that the crime rate is inversely related to the severity of the punishment imposed and positively related to the benefits to be gained, which is to say that punishment does indeed deter crime.)[40] It may or may not be the case that irrationality plays a greater role in criminal behavior than it does in economic, but Ehrlich assumed that at least some murders are committed by persons who expect to gain more from murdering than from not murdering and who, before they act, calculate the probable costs as well as the probable gains. The gains appear in his model of the "murder supply function" in the form of annual statistics respecting the unemployment rate, the labor force participation rate, and an estimate of real per capita income; which is to say, he made the assumption that the gains to be won by murder will be related to the economic factors expressed in these statistics. The probable costs appear as statistics, from the same years, respecting the probability of murderers being apprehended, convicted, and executed. With these he included statistics of the percentage of the population in the age group 14–25 in each of the years studied, the assumption being (and it is a well-founded assumption) that this group has a higher propensity to commit murders. His hypothesis was that the murder rate is dependent on these eight variables, and this dependence is expressed mathematically in a set of simultaneous equations. Appropriate estimation techniques were then used to obtain numerical values of the parameters in the model.

It is a complex technique. (Some idea of the complexities involved in this kind of study may be glimpsed in the fact that Ehrlich found it necessary to take account of—which is to say, express mathematically—the possibility that the number of murders may have been diminished systematically over time due to a continual improvement in medical technology, with the result that what would have been a murder in an earlier year was—because the victim's life was saved—merely an attempted murder in a later year.)[41] But the complexity is a consequence of the attempt to avoid the shortcomings of the simpler studies, shortcomings that made their findings inconclusive. For example, Ehrlich hypothesized that an increase in executions would have two opposite effects: fewer murders, because of a perception of a greater probability of execution, and more murders, because of a perception of a smaller probability of conviction (due to the refusal of juries to convict when execution is the prescribed penalty). He was also able to deal with another problem left unresolved by the earlier studies, namely, the necessity to distinguish between a decline in murders attributable to incapacitation of the convicted murderer (an executed murderer is completely incapacitated) and a decline attributable to the deterrence of murders by others. In the period studied by Ehrlich, the number of murders and the murder rate had risen dramatically while the number of executions fell off to zero. Once changes in the other dependent variables are taken into account, however, Ehrlich can conclude only that the one *may* have been a cause of the other. As he put it, "one cannot reject the hypothesis that punishment in general, and execution in particular, exert a unique deterrent effect on potential murderers."[42] Or, "an additional execution per year over the period in question may have resulted, on average, in 7 or 8 fewer murders."[43]

Ehrlich's study was described, in a reply brief quickly filed by counsel for the petitioner in the *Fowler* case, as one "riddled with theoretical and technical errors that render its conclusions meaningless. Despite the complicated array of mathematical symbols and econometric terminology, the [study] is a creation of mere arbitrary assumptions, misleading summarizations, and reckless inferences."[44] These are obviously serious charges and, even though made in a lawyer's brief, cannot be summarily dismissed, especially when the brief depends heavily on a paper written by two econometricians whose credentials are, in principle, the equal of Ehrlich's.[45] Some of the criticism is directed against multiple regression analysis itself and some against Ehrlich's application of it. In the latter category are criticisms of the data he used, of his failure to control for the length of prison sentences imposed on convicted murderers, and of his assumption that the relations among the posited eight independent variables and the murder rate remain unchanged throughout the country. In the former category, the critics, while conceding the superiority of multiple regression analysis in controlling for the factors that are thought to be statistically related to a described condition (for example, the murder rate), it is, needless to say, incapable of controlling for a factor omitted from the model, and the fact of this omission can lead to serious misstatements. This is said to be especially likely when data are drawn from widely separated points in time. One of his critics carried out a multivariate regression analysis on cross-section data for the census years 1950 and 1960 (instead of country-wide data for a number of years), and found executions to have no deterrent effect beyond that achieved by imprisonment.[46] He concluded that it could not be proved that executions deter murder; on the other hand (and this concession may be one consequence of Ehrlich's work), he said it cannot be proved that executions do *not* deter murder. "Proof is simply beyond the capacity of empirical social science."[47]

In a reply to his critics, Ehrlich emphasized that he never claimed that his research "settles the issue of the deterrent effect of capital punishment," but he defended his work as superior to any by his critics, either before or after his own. "The fact is that I have learned of no single error in either my theoretical analysis or the statistical methodology used to implement the theory."[48] And, surely, some of the criticism leveled against him is ill-conceived, or petty to an extent not usually encountered in a scholarly journal. David Baldus and James Cole charge him with a failure to "focus on the relevant policy question."

The precise question now facing the Supreme Court is whether capital punishment must be abolished, not whether its use should be increased or decreased assuming it is retained. For some purposes, it may be of interest to investigate the effects of increasing the number of

executions in retentionist jurisdictions. But in the debate over abolition, the essential question is the effect of changing from a retentionist
to an abolitionist jurisdiction. Sellin's approach is directly addressed to
this policy choice, and Ehrlich's is not.[49]

But if Ehrlich is right, the effect of "changing from a retentionist
to an abolitionist jurisdiction" may be a marked increase in the
number of murders. He may be wrong but his findings are
certainly not irrelevant to the "policy choice" to be made.

There have been other studies critical of Ehrlich's work.
The work is too powerful and its conclusions too significant to
be ignored. Some of these studies are discussed in a recent
article by Hans Zeisel, who especially praises an unpublished
paper, which I have not seen, by Brian Forst. The power of
Forst's paper, he says, derives from an analysis of changes (in
the number of executions and murders) *"both* over time and
across jurisdictions."[50] No sooner was this said than Ehrlich
appeared in print again, this time with a major new study
using cross-sectional data; its results, he insisted, "reinforce"
his earlier time series study.[51] Thus, although the deterrence
issue may not yet be resolved, this at least can be said: Ehrlich
succeeded in reopening the question, and no one can now say
what was regularly said earlier, namely, that it is *known* that
the death penalty is not a more effective deterrent. As even
Passell and Taylor put it in a recent article, "on the basis of
Ehrlich's research, it is prudent neither to accept nor reject the
hypothesis that capital punishment deters murder."[52] The
question is, what conclusion do we draw from this? Or, if we
cannot resolve this question of deterrence, which "policy
choice" do we make?

In the 1976 Canadian debates, Prime Minister Trudeau said
to the House of Commons that if the bill to abolish the death
penalty were defeated, "some people will certainly hang," and
he threatened the opponents of the abolition bill with responsibility for those hangings. Yet, if Ehrlich is right, abolition of
capital punishment may result in the deaths of as many as eight

persons for every murderer who is not executed. The "policy choice," then, turns in part on the answer to this question: whose life should be of more concern to the law, that of the Quebec cabinet minister Pierre Laporte or those of the FLQ *(Front de Libération du Québec)* terrorists who garroted him with baling wire and stuffed his body into the trunk of an automobile? The life of seventeen-year-old Kathleen McKenzie or that of her murderer, Ivan Horvat, who, after killing her, smeared her body with agricultural lime in what the police said was a crude attempt to conceal her identity? (Within a few months of his statement to the House of Commons, Trudeau's government, in an effort to put an end to a riot in a maximum security prison, was negotiating with a committee headed by Horvat. The impropriety of this apparently never occurred to any member of the government.)[53] Or, for an American example, the life of Henry Jarrette or the lives of his victims? (Jarrette was a double murderer, but he was not executed. Instead, he was given a long-term prison sentence and then allowed to leave the prison in order to attend the state convention of the Junior Chamber of Commerce in Raleigh, North Carolina. He was a duly elected officer of the prison chapter of the state Jaycees, so why shouldn't he be allowed to attend the convention? While in Raleigh, he eluded his guard and escaped. Two days later he seized a sixteen-year-old black girl, bound her hands behind her back, threw her in a car he had stolen, drove off to a secluded place in the woods, raped her, threw her back in the car, and drove back to town; there he stabbed and killed a sixteen-year-old white boy who had the misfortune to be sitting at the wheel of another car to which Jarrette took a fancy.)[54] If the death penalty is permitted, people like Horvat and Jarrette "will certainly [or will probably] hang"; and if it is not permitted, and if Ehrlich is right, a larger number of people —and in this case, innocent people—will probably be murdered.

CRIME WITHOUT PUNISHMENT

One of the frequently used arguments against the death penalty is that murder is a crime that cannot be deterred. It is insisted that, beyond all others, murder is a crime of passion, a crime committed by wife against husband or husband against wife, or under the influence of alcohol by friend against erstwhile friend, and, on the whole, the statistics bear this out. Whereas persons tend overwhelmingly to commit their armed robberies against strangers, they tend to murder their friends, lovers, and acquaintances and to do so in the familiar surroundings of the home.[55] Acting in a fit of passion, murderers are incapable of a rational calculation of costs and benefits, and, therefore, it is argued, incapable of being deterred by the threat of capital punishment.

But the same argument leads to the conclusion that they are incapable of being deterred by the threat of any punishment; and if deterrence is the only purpose of punishment, and if no punishment can deter the typical murderer, then it would seem that the law is wasting its time and our money when it punishes him. Rehabilitation (even if it were possible) is irrelevant here: a murderer is the least likely of criminals to repeat his crime— Henry Jarrette is an exception to the rule—so nothing is accomplished by incapacitating him, either by executing him or imprisoning him. The conclusion to which this argument leads is not merely that murderers ought not to be executed, but that they ought not even be imprisoned, or, for that matter, arrested. In fact, murder ought not to be considered a criminal offense.

In addition to leading to conclusions that no sane man will accept, this argument fails to prove what it sets out to prove. The fact that murder tends to be a crime of passion does not prove that murder cannot be deterred by the threat of severe punishment. It is possible that precisely because of the severe

104

punishments prescribed, murders tend to be committed, on the whole, *only* by those unable to weigh the possible costs against the probable benefits. Others, even those who stand to gain by murdering (and most of us are in this category), are deterred by the costs, or may be deterred by them. At least, the crime of passion argument does nothing to cast doubt on the possibility that we are deterred by the threat of punishment. Who would be so bold as to predict that the murder rate would not rise if murderers were not punished in any way? Besides, we know as a fact that the number of murders tends to rise with the crime rate in general—and not only in America—which suggests that a significant number of murders are being committed "in cold blood" by persons other than jealous husbands or forsaken lovers. Interestingly enough, this proves to be true.

In 1966, 16.3 percent of all murders were what the FBI refers to as "spouse-spouse" murders; this proportion dropped steadily until, in 1974, it reached 12.1 percent. More or less the same thing happened respecting the proportions of murders committed by parents, "other relatives," and those involved in "romantic triangles and lovers quarrels." The proportion of killings arising out of "other arguments" (a category that probably includes barroom brawls) remained essentially unchanged (40.9 percent in 1966 and 43.2 percent in 1974). The one category that showed a marked increase is "known felony murders." These constituted 14.8 percent of the total in 1966 and 22.2 percent in 1974.[56] More murders and a greater proportion of murders are being committed by professional criminals in "cold blood" in the course of committing other felonies. In New York City, 1,645 homicides were committed in 1975, more than a third of which were classified as "stranger murders," the highest rate in the country. Such murder cases are more difficult to solve than other kinds, and we can expect that as the proportion of them rises, the proportion of cases "cleared" or solved will drop and that the proportion of murderers punished will also drop. New York police managed to make arrests in only 64.5

percent of its homicide cases in 1975, which was the lowest "clearance" rate among the large American cities.[57] My point is a simple one: if crime in general could be deterred more effectively, murder in particular might also be deterred more effectively. Crime in general is not now being deterred because, compared to the amount of crime, almost no one is being punished, and almost no one is being punished partly because our judges do not believe in punishment. They still believe in rehabilitation.

We know about the amount and rate of crime from the FBI's *Uniform Crime Reports,* and while these annual reports are less reliable than we would like them to be, there is no reason to believe that they are less reliable this year than last, or less reliable last year than the year before. They show that there are fluctuations in the crime rate from year to year that defy explanation—for example, there is no apparent explanation of the decline in the number of murders from 20,600 in 1974 to 18,-780 in 1976—but they also show consistencies—for example, we know that an appreciable part of the increase in the rate of crime in recent decades is attributable to the disproportionate growth, during this period, of the younger age group which, we know as a fact, commits a disproportionate part of the crime. The *Reports* show that the per capita crime rate (crimes per 100,000 population) declined slightly in 1976, compared with the previous year, but that in 1977 it appears to have increased again, which is consistent with the secular trend.[58] There is little comfort to be derived from the statistics.

There were, for example, 11,304,800 index crimes known to have been committed in the United States during 1976,* an increase of 236 percent over 1960; in this same period, the crime rate jumped from 1,875.8 per 100,000 population to 5,-266.4 per 100,000, an increase of 181 percent. Of particular

*Index crimes as defined by the FBI comprise (1) murder and nonnegligent manslaughter, (2) forcible rape, (3) aggravated assault, (4) robbery, (5) burglary, (6) larceny-theft, and (7) motor vehicle theft.

interest here is the number of murders: 18,780 in 1976 and 9,060 in 1960. This is an increase of 107 percent, and an increase in the per capita murder rate of 73 percent. In this same period, the rate of forcible rapes increased 178 percent; robberies, 226 percent; aggravated assaults, 168 percent; burglaries, 185 percent; larcenies, 184 percent; and motor vehicle thefts, 145 percent.[59]

Thus, the public's perception that crime is a worsening problem is borne out by the statistics; so too is the public's perception that not much is being done about it. The police manage to make an arrest in approximately 20 percent of the cases, but only a small portion of those arrested are actually convicted in the courts, and a still smaller portion punished. The figures are as follows (per 100 index crimes committed):[60]

Arrests	19.4
Persons charged	17.5
Persons guilty as charged	5.0
Persons guilty of lesser offense	0.8
Persons acquitted or dismissed	2.4
Juveniles referred to juvenile courts	5.8

Thus, for every 100 index crimes reported to the police there are 5.8 convictions, not counting the convictions in the juvenile courts. The number of these is not reported, but if we assume that these courts convict half the offenders referred to them, the total conviction rate is 8.7 percent; which is to say, that for every 100 index crimes known to have been committed there are 8.7 convictions. This means that an estimated 91.3 percent of the reported crimes go unpunished. But the situation is actually worse because most crimes are not reported.

This fact had long been suspected and now, thanks to the victimization surveys conducted by the Census Bureau for the Law Enforcement Assistance Administration, it has been verified. Information in these victimization reports is obtained from twice-yearly interviews with a national representative sample of 60,000 households and 15,000 businesses, who are asked to report the specific crimes committed against them during the period covered. Except that murder is not included, the crimes surveyed are roughly equivalent to the FBI's index crimes. What we learn, among other things, is that there is marked disparity between the number of crimes reported to the police (and recorded by the FBI) and the number of crimes committed. Thus, for example, in 1973 the FBI reported the rate of forcible rape to be 24.3 per 100,000, and the National Crime Survey reported it to be 100, or four times greater; and the robbery rate as recorded by the FBI was 198.4 and, as reported by the victims, 690.[61] In a press release of 15 April 1974, the LEAA Administrator at that time, Donald E. Santarelli, indicated that only 37 percent of the crimes suffered by Detroiters were reported to the police, a figure that was not out of line with the survey results in other cities covered in the report.[62] (The figures mentioned were 36 percent for Chicago, 34 percent for Los Angeles, 47 percent for New York, and 20 percent for Philadelphia.) National figures reported in 1976 disclosed that the proportion of unreported crimes ranged from 74 percent (household larcenies) to 32 percent (vehicle thefts). If, then, we assume that only 40 percent of the crimes committed are reported to the police on the whole, the number of index crimes committed in 1974 was 25,480,000, or two-and-a-half times greater than the number reported to the police.[63] This means that if there are 8.7 convictions for every 100 recorded index crimes, there are only 3.48 convictions for every 100 crimes committed, which is to say that 96.5 percent of the crimes committed go unpunished (assuming, for the moment, that everyone convicted is punished).

This raises the question of what is meant by punishment. In Gallup polls the public was asked whether, in general, the courts "deal too harshly, or not harshly enough with criminals," and the responses are reported in the following table:[64]

	Too harshly	Not enough	About right	No opinion
1965: April	2	48	34	16
1968: February	2	63	19	16
1969: January	2	75	13	10

A Harris poll, asking a similar question in 1970, reported that 64 percent of the respondents thought that the courts were "too lenient" in dealing with criminals. This is surely one of those areas where the public has merely a vague perception of the facts as to which it is asked to make a pronouncement—who knows what "too harshly" means, or "about right," and how many persons are in possession of the facts concerning sentencing?—yet the perception may be accurate for all that. In 1973, for example, a total of 34,983 persons were sentenced by the federal courts; of this total, 15,025, or 43 percent, were put on probation and 1,866, or 5.3 percent, were fined. In addition, 2,883, or 8.2 percent, were given what in federal law is called a "split sentence," which means a sentence of six months or less in a "jail-type institution" followed by a term of probation.[65] So far as I have been able to determine, this pattern of sentencing prevails in the state courts as well; according to one recent study, "over half of all convicted offenders in the United States are placed on probation,"[66] and a decade ago California reported that 48.9 percent of all felony defendants were so treated.[67] Nor was probation confined to relatively minor offenses. Of those convicted of the seven index crimes (or their equivalents in federal law), 2,874, or 37 percent, were placed on probation by federal courts in 1971.[68] These figures gain additional significance when viewed with those concerning defendants who have prior criminal records. This information was available for 23,390 of the 32,103 persons convicted in federal courts in 1971, the last year for which we have the statistics, and of these 14,489, or 62 percent, had prior criminal records.[69] The probability is strong that probation is being granted to a significant number of defendants with prior criminal records.

Indeed, in particular jurisdictions where this subject has been studied in detail, this has been proved to be the case.

For example, Martin A. Levin of Brandeis University found in a study of the Pittsburgh Common Pleas Court in 1966 that well over one-half the white males convicted of burglary, grand larceny, indecent assault, or possession of narcotics, and who had a prior record, were placed on probation; nearly one-half of the two-time losers convicted of aggravated assault were also placed on probation, as were more than one-fourth of those convicted of robbery. In Wisconsin, Dean V. Babst and John W. Mannering found that 63 per cent of the adult males convicted of a felony during 1954–1959 who had previously been convicted of another felony were placed on probation, and 41 per cent of those with two or more felony convictions were given probation for the subsequent offense. In Los Angeles, only 6 percent of those charged with burglary, who had a serious prior record, were sent to prison; only 12 per cent of those charged with burglary who had already been in prison were sent back.[70]

But perhaps the most revealing information is to be found in prisoner statistics. Despite the fact that the number of index crimes known to the police increased from 3,363,700 in 1960 to 8,666,200 in 1973, an increase of 158 percent, there were fewer persons in federal and state prisons in 1973 than in 1960.[71] Not until 1974 did the number increase to the point where it exceeded the 1960 total.[72] There were many more criminals, but they were not in prison. If we exclude probation from the category of punishment, we arrive at this conclusion: 3.4 convictions for every 100 crimes committed, and half of those convicted are punished. Hence, 98.3 percent of the crimes committed go unpunished. This, surely, is a situation that Hobbes and Beccaria did not foresee when they first advanced the proposition that the purpose of punishment is to instill fear of the sovereign's laws. Rather than fearing the laws, American criminals have good reason to regard them with contempt.

Judges are reluctant to punish because the idea of punishment fell into disrepute in prestigious legal circles. Part of a lawyer's, and especially a judge's, education has been that the use of punishment should be avoided. The American Law Institute's Model Penal Code (which is one of the most influential legal documents of the past few decades) instructs judges to avoid imprisoning a convicted criminal except (1) to incapacitate him, (2) to rehabilitate him, or (3) when necessary to avoid depreciation of the seriousness of his offense. Thus, withholding a sentence of imprisonment is to be the rule and imprisonment is to be the exception, and from the sentencing section itself one might conclude that no one should be imprisoned in order to deter others from committing similar offenses.[73] The same principle animated the Council of Judges of the National Council on Crime and Delinquency when, even in the second edition of their Model Sentencing Act (published in 1972), they provided that, except for dangerous offenders, "persons convicted of crime shall be dealt with in accordance with their potential for rehabilitation, considering their individual characteristics, circumstances and needs." In the comment accompanying this article, they acknowledge that while "some persons, including a few members of the Council of Judges, maintain that punishment *per se* has a proper place in a sentence, the consensus is that the term 'punishment' standing alone is vague."[74] (This sentence is itself vague, but its implication seems clear enough: the Council of Judges is persuaded that criminals ought not to be punished.)

The sentencing practices of judges have recently been subjected to a powerful and informed attack by a federal trial judge, who refers to the unchecked and sweeping powers given to judges as "terrifying and intolerable for a society that professes devotion to the rule of law";[75] but even in the course of demonstrating the injustices of the sentencing system, he, too, reveals his attachment to the sentiment that underlies it. He is firmly convinced, he says, that not only are too many persons sentenced to prison terms that are far too long (an opinion that can be supported with persuasive evidence), but that "too many people" are being imprisoned.[76] Hence, he, too, even as he complains of statutes providing for indeterminate sentences, calls for "creative thought" to be given to rehabilitation programs involving "probation, work release, halfway houses," and the like, as if there were some reason to believe that rehabilitation works (but he knows there is none).[77]

Admittedly, there are gross disparities in sentencing, but the evidence reviewed above suggests that for every "hanging judge" who imposes excessively severe sentences, there are several whose illusions or softness cause them to err in the opposite direction. The fact is that a "shockingly large number [of criminals] go unpunished," as a recent task force report puts it, and that this state of affairs has "seriously affected the deterrent value of criminal sanctions."[78] How could it be otherwise when, as I calculate it, 98.3 percent of the serious crimes go unpunished? In this situation, the question is not why so many persons commit crimes *but why so many persons do not commit crimes,* when, from a certain point of view, it is obviously in their interest to do so. They are laboring under an illusion if they are being restrained by the fear of punishment. The possibility of being punished is altogether remote; it is remote not only because of the difficulty of catching criminals but because of the unwillingness of the courts to punish them when caught and convicted, and also because of the difficulty of convicting them.*

THE COURT PROBLEM

From the beginning criminology has asserted that if punishment has any capacity to deter crimes (and in the beginning there was no doubt about this), it consisted in its certainty and

---

*I have no doubt that the prospect of being arrested alone is sufficient to deter the typical law-abiding citizen. He regards arrest as shameful.

in the promptness of its imposition. Beccaria made these two arguments in consecutive chapters of his treatise. "One of the greatest curbs on crime," he said, "is not the cruelty of punishments, but their infallibility"; and the "more promptly and the more closely punishment follows upon the commission of a crime, the more just and useful it will be." He therefore, in true Hobbesian fashion, urged magistrates to be more vigilant and judges "inexorable." But in the United States today, punishment is neither infallible nor prompt, which is why the criminal justice system is described even by sympathetic observers as a failure "unable to protect the community from crime."[79]

The system is characterized by delay, apparently unnecessary delay, at every stage. The average British defendant is brought to trial within 12.1 weeks if he is not in custody and within 8.3 weeks if he is in custody, and the British complain that this period is excessively long, much longer than fifteen years earlier;[80] yet the President's Commission on Law Enforcement and Administration of Justice, in one of its task force reports in 1967, set these times as targets to be achieved by American courts. In actuality, the waiting periods are much longer. The task force saw no reason why a criminal case could not be disposed of within three months, but a recent study by Lewis Katz found that the average urban court in America requires nine months to dispose of a case.[81] In another study, Macklin Fleming, a justice of the California court of appeals, provided the following example of the law's delay in what he described as a routine California criminal case.[82] The defendant was apprehended in the act of burglary—caught red-handed, as the saying goes—on 7 December 1968, after which the following proceedings took place:

1968

30 *December.* Information filed charging sundry robberies, burglaries, rapes, kidnapping, and sexual offenses.

1969

6 *January.* Defendant arraigned and pleaded not guilty.

3 *February.* Information amended to charge prior offenses. Trial continued to 4 March.

4 *February.* Arraignment and plea continued to 10 February.

10 *February.* Arraignment and plea continued to 13 February.

13 *February.* Defendant arraigned and pleaded not guilty. Trial date remained 4 March.

28 *February.* On defendant's motion trial continued to 2 April.

2 *April.* On defendant's motion trial continued to 24 April.

24 *April.* On defendant's motion that his counsel was elsewhere engaged, trial continued to 1 May.

1 *May.* On defendant's motion trial continued to 9 May.

9 *May.* On defendant's motion that his counsel was elsewhere engaged, trial continued to 14 May.

14 *May.* On defendant's motion that counsel was elsewhere engaged, trial continued to 15 May.

15 *May.* On defendant's motion trial continued to 20 May.

20 *May.* Defendant pleaded guilty to three counts of the information. Probation and sentence set for 13 June.

13 *June.* Mentally disordered sex offender proceedings initiated, and proceedings continued to 10 July.

10 *July.* Defendant's motion to withdraw guilty plea granted, and not-guilty plea reinstated. Cause continued to 18 July for trial setting.

18 *July.* On motion of defendant, cause continued to 1 August for trial setting.

1 *August.* On motion of defendant, cause continued to 8 August for trial setting.

8 *August.* On motion of defendant, cause continued to 29 August.

29 *August.* Prosecution moves to vacate order reinstating defendant's not-guilty plea. On motion of defendant cause continued to 5 September.

5 *September.* By stipulation cause continued to 1 October.

1 *October.* Prosecution's motion to vacate order reinstating not-guilty plea denied. Cause continued to 8 October for trial setting.

8 *October.* Trial set for 2 December.

13 *November.* Hearing on defendant's discovery motion; motion granted in part.

26 *November.* Defendant's motion to dismiss two kidnapping counts

granted as to one. Trial date of 2 December vacated, and cause continued to 3 December for trial setting.

3 December. Cause set for trial on 21 January 1970.

1970

21 January. Defendant's motion to relieve deputy public defender is denied. Defendant's motion to suppress evidence continued to 22 January.

22 January. Cause continued to 23 January.

23 January. Hearing on motion to suppress evidence continued to 26 January.

26 January. Motion to suppress evidence in part. Hearing held on motion to dismiss lineup evidence. Later, motion is denied. Trial continued to 27 January.

27 January. Trial begins.

9 February. Jury returned verdicts of guilty.

4 March. Judgment and sentence.[83]

Defendants (even, apparently, those in custody) favor delay because it enhances their chances of having the charges against them reduced or even dropped: witnesses may disappear, become discouraged, forget, or even die. Defense attorneys favor delay because it serves as a means to enable them to collect their fees (Katz reports that this is a common practice[84]), because it enables them to accept more cases than they could handle under a more rigid calendar, and because, when lawyers act as court-appointed attorneys, the fee structure discourages their going to trial.[85] But the law-abiding community is penalized by delays; unfortunately, as Katz says, this community is simply not adequately represented in the courts, and the courts permit delay. "Between defendants and lawyers—and it must be kept in mind that judges and prosecutors are lawyers too—the procedures are being neatly emasculated to ensure that only their respective interests are protected."[86] (Katz himself is a lawyer.) There is a need for more judges and other court personnel, and a good deal of effort is being exerted to make the courts more efficient by such means as the use of computers to assist in record keeping and scheduling and new management techniques, but the problem is not simply one of inefficiency and will not be solved unless the use of new techniques and devices is combined with a change of attitude on the part of judges. "Simply stated, the public has the right to demand that courts function in the interest of society and not as a private club for lawyers."[87] The aphorism, justice delayed is justice denied, would appear to have been coined with the innocent defendant in mind; with respect to the guilty, justice delayed has the effect of diminishing the chances of conviction and punishment and, therefore, of deterring crime.

But trial judges are not solely responsible for the inefficiency of our criminal justice system. Some cases are tried—and tried and tried—but final judgment does not typically follow immediately upon the conclusion of the trial. When a case begins with a search or arrest warrant or a wire-tap, or when it depends on a confession, and when the defendant enjoys the assistance of assiduous or pertinacious counsel, the opportunities for avoiding final judgment are almost limitless. Fleming says such a defendant may be able to "postpone the day of final judgment to Armageddon,"[88] and for this he blames the Supreme Court, and particularly the Court under Chief Justice Earl Warren.

A defendant about to be tried in a state court may begin by asking a federal court to enjoin the state prosecution on the ground that the statute under which he is to be tried is unconstitutional on its face or is one whose enforcement would have a "chilling" effect on the exercise of a claimed constitutional right.[89] Or he may file a motion in which he claims that evidence to be used against him was improperly seized or, for another example, that an arrest warrant was issued without probable cause, and, if his motion is denied by the trial judge, he may launch a collateral attack by asking another court to issue a writ of prohibition; if he fails to get it, he may appeal that judgment to a still higher court. Fleming calls these techniques "preconviction shuttles."

If the defendant is nevertheless finally convicted, he can begin the postconviction relief journey through the state's appellate system and then to the Supreme Court of the United States. Even if he loses in each of these courts and is finally imprisoned, he is not yet without remedy. The next step is one made more readily available by the Supreme Court some twenty years ago when it affirmed the right of a state defendant, whose conviction has already been affirmed on direct appeal, to apply to a federal district court for habeas corpus. If this is denied, he can then appeal the denial to the federal Court of Appeals and, finally, to the Supreme Court of the United States again. The number of habeas corpus petitions filed annually by state prisoners now exceeds 12,000, some 2,000 of which reach the Supreme Court.[90]

It is inevitable that procedures so solicitous of a defendant's interests will produce cases that make criminal justice appear ridiculous, and Fleming provides an example of one:

Six persons died as a result of the throwing by Bates and Chavez of five gallons of gasoline and lighted matches into the Mecca Bar in Los Angeles on the night of 4 April 1957. Bates, Chavez, and others had been denied service at the bar and ejected for creating a disturbance. Swearing to get even, they purchased five gallons of gasoline in an open bucket, returned to the bar, threw the gasoline on the floor, and then threw a book of lighted matches on the gasoline. In the resulting flash fire five persons were killed by carbon monoxide, and a sixth was killed by asphyxia and burns. A jury convicted Bates and Chavez of six counts of murder and one count of arson, and death sentences were imposed. The judgments were affirmed in 1958 by the California Supreme Court, and hearings were denied in 1959 by the United States Supreme Court.

Collateral review immediately began in the federal courts with the filing by Bates and Chavez in 1959 of petitions for habeas corpus. Their petitions were denied by the district court, but in June 1960 the federal court of appeals ordered the district court to consider two issues —whether the written transcripts of orally recorded statements of the defendants were, as claimed, grossly inaccurate, and whether the photographs of the bodies of the victims were, as claimed, so excessively gruesome that their use amounted to prejudicial error.

Thereafter the district court found that the transcripts were substantially accurate and that the photographs were not excessively gruesome and denied the petitions for habeas corpus. This denial was affirmed by the federal court of appeals in 1962, and a hearing was denied by the United States Supreme Court.

In 1963, after an unsuccessful petition for a writ of habeas corpus in the California Supreme Court, Bates and Chavez filed new petitions for habeas corpus in the federal district court. Hearings on those petitions were held during 1964, and in June 1966 the petitions were denied.

Meanwhile the Governor of California commuted Bates' sentence to life imprisonment without possibility of parole and commuted Chavez's sentence to life imprisonment.

In 1967 the federal court of appeals affirmed the district court's denial of habeas corpus. But in 1968 the United States Supreme Court vacated the decision of the court of appeals and remanded the case for further consideration in the light of two recent Supreme Court decisions: *Burgett* v. *Texas,* a 1967 ruling that a defendant's earlier conviction while unrepresented by counsel cannot be used to support guilt or to enhance punishment, and *Bruton* v. *United States,* a 1968 holding that the admission of incriminating extrajudicial statements of a codefendant violates the defendant's right to cross-examination even though the jury has been instructed to disregard the statements with respect to the defendant himself.

In November 1971 the federal district court, in which the case had made its home for more than a decade, determined that neither the use of prior convictions to impeach the veracity of Bates' testimony nor the use of statements of codefendants in the cause amounted to prejudicial error, and the court again denied the petitions for habeas corpus. In 1973 an appeal from this denial was pending in the federal court of appeals.[91]

Since Fleming wrote, the federal Court of Appeals upheld the denial of the petition and Chavez (for some reason, not Bates) appealed to the Supreme Court, which also ruled against him.[92] There, perhaps, after seventeen years, the matter will come to rest, although not necessarily. It is always possible (although, since the advent of the Burger court, not likely) that the Supreme Court will announce a new constitutional rule of criminal procedure and then apply the rule retroactively, thus making it possible for Bates and Chavez to have a new trial and, assuming the witnesses are still available to testify and the evidence has not been destroyed, if they are again convicted, to begin the appeals process once again. The retroactive application of the rule of *Gideon* v. *Wainwright*[93] (according to which every indigent felony defendant in the state courts is, as a matter of federal constitutional law, entitled to the assistance of court-appointed counsel) had consequences that serve to illustrate the point. Over 6,000 prisoners in Florida alone (where the case originated) filed postconviction motions,[94] which led either to new trials or the release of the prisoners. It is possible that Bates and Chavez will benefit from some such decision in the future. On sixteen occasions (as I count them) the state and federal courts examined this trial and, finally, pronounced it a fair one *at the time it took place,* but it is not impossible that in the future it will be found to be unfair according to some standard still to be set. Yet, as Fleming says, it has never been controverted "that Bates threw the gasoline on the floor of the Mecca Bar, that Chavez threw a book of lighted matches on the gasoline, and that six persons died in the ensuing holocaust."[95] Punishment in America, even after conviction, is neither infallible nor prompt.

In our present situation, it is easy to find fault with our manner of conducting criminal trials and to overlook the faults in other systems. It is, for example, deplorable that so much time is spent impaneling an American jury (five weeks in the trial of the notorious Charles Manson and "family"), and it is easy to envy the British and Canadians who manage to impanel a jury in a matter of minutes or hours. But there is another side to this, as a recent Canadian example serves to illustrate. In the province of Manitoba the names of prospective jurors are taken at random from the voters' lists and the jurors are not routinely questioned before appearing for duty. Nor are defense counsel permitted to interrogate them in order, ostensibly at least, to discover whether they have opinions on the case. Fair enough, one is inclined to say: much more efficient than allowing all those peremptory challenges and evidentiary hearings on the composition of juries, with their allegations of discrimination of one sort or another. Unfortunately, a recent attempted-murder trial in Manitoba ended in a mistrial when, after three days of testimony, it was discovered that two of the jurors could not understand English and a third was so deaf that by his own admission he was able to hear only about half of what had been said in the trial.[96] That, at least, is not likely to happen in an American trial.

One must also avoid minimizing the evils the various Warren Court–sponsored rules were designed to correct. Other free countries manage to live without the exclusionary rule, for example, according to which evidence obtained illegally is inadmissible in the trial,[97] or the somewhat similar *Miranda* rule[98] respecting the inadmissibility of confessions obtained without informing the suspect that he may remain silent and is entitled to have counsel present, and so on; but these other countries also have more effective methods of preventing police misbehavior. No federal official in the United States has an authority over local police equivalent to that enjoyed by the British home secretary, for example. The Supreme Court made the exclusionary rule into a rule of constitutional law only because there seemed to be no other way of getting the police to behave properly.

Yet, the rule has been of no use in this regard. As even Leonard Levy admits (and Levy is one of the Warren Court's strongest supporters), the impact of the rule "misses the police and falls upon prosecutors." The police can continue their illegal searches, seizures, and interrogations without suffering any penalty deriving from the exclusionary rule (the prosecutors suffer the penalty); indeed, the rule cannot conceivably reach those cases where a remedy is most evidently needed: illegal searches involving innocent persons. In such cases, no evidence is seized and, therefore, none can be excluded.[99] The consequence is we have a rule of constitutional law that does a good deal of harm—making it more difficult to obtain convictions, delaying the progress of trials, and proliferating appeals —without doing any good.

The same criticism can be made of the generosity with which we allow appeals in criminal cases—from the state courts to the Supreme Court of the United States, then from the lower federal courts to the Supreme Court again. Yet, as Fleming demonstrates, the proponents of these federal postconviction remedies have not been able to uncover a single innocent person saved by their use.[100] There can be no quarrel with the proposition that there must be procedures designed to supervise trials to the end of protecting the innocent and guaranteeing the rights of even the guilty defendant; the disagreement arises on the question of how much supervision we can afford without jeopardizing the criminal justice system. After all, there is a difference between the rights of a defendant and his interest. His rights are described in the Constitution and in the rules of criminal procedure; his interest is to escape punishment.

Justice Brennan once said, in a case concerning the availability of federal postconviction remedies, that "conventional notions of finality of litigation have no place where life or liberty is at stake and infringement of constitutional rights is alleged."[101] It is instructive to calculate how often this occurs. Liberty is at stake in every case in which the accused has been found guilty and sentenced to a term of imprisonment; allegations of infringement of a constitutional right are made in almost all cases appealed. How many cases are appealed? Leaving aside the cases tried in state courts (for which the relevant statistics are unavailable), in 1974 a total of 36,229 persons were found guilty in the United States district courts. Of these, 29,843 entered a plea of guilty and 6,386 were convicted after trial before judge or jury. Of this latter group, 4,067, or 64 percent, filed appeals in the United States Courts of Appeals.[102]

Justice Brennan's statement means, then, that conventional notions of finality of litigation have no place in the typical, or "conventional," federal criminal case.

Presumably the British are as determined as we are to prevent illegal imprisonments and convictions of innocent persons, but they nevertheless have designed a judicial system in which, by our standards, appeals are rarely taken. In 1974, a total of 374,918 persons were found guilty of indictable offenses in the courts of England and Wales; there is no way of knowing from what has been published how many of these entered pleas of guilty and how many were found guilty after trial, but of the total, only 4,481 applied for leave to appeal, or approximately 1.2 percent.[103] The parallel American figure is 11.2 percent, or about ten times greater. If the British courts were suddenly to adopt rules of procedure that had the effect of increasing the number of appeals tenfold, the results would surely be the collapse of their criminal justice system; and we ought not be surprised that a gradual imposition of these rules in the United States has contributed to the impairment of the capacity of our criminal courts to perform the primary function for which they were created: to determine the guilty and bring them to justice.[104] This, however, was not how the Warren Court viewed the primary function of the criminal courts.

No judge better characterized the Warren Court and the spirit guiding its criminal procedure cases than William O. Douglas, who once said that any doubt that arises in a criminal case should be resolved in favor of the liberty of the citizen. We have become so accustomed to such statements that they appear unexceptionable, as simply stating the justice of the matter in a free country. But the statement embodies a pernicious principle. Before agreeing that *any* doubt should be resolved in the defendant's favor, it is useful to examine the case in which Douglas made the statement. A person named Downum and three others were charged with mail theft and with forging (and "uttering") checks stolen from the mails. The three codefendants pleaded guilty, but Downum elected to stand trial. The case was called and both sides announced they were ready to proceed. The jury was selected, sworn, and immediately instructed to return at 2.00 P.M. the same afternoon. During the recess, the prosecutor learned that he had been misinformed, that his key witness was not in fact present; he informed the judge during the recess and, when the court reconvened, he immediately asked that the jury be discharged. His motion was granted. Two days later, a second jury was impaneled and Downum, after complaining of double jeopardy, was convicted. The Court of Appeals affirmed, but the Supreme Court reversed and Downum was set free.[105]

Now the Fifth Amendment provides that no person should be subject for the same offense "to be twice put in jeopardy of life or limb," and it does so in order to prevent the harassment of an accused by successive prosecutions or to prevent declarations of a mistrial intended to afford the prosecution a more favorable opportunity to convict in a subsequent trial. Douglas made these points. But he also admitted that the established law of double jeopardy did not forbid all discontinuances of a trial necessitated by the absence of witnesses. Each case must be judged on its facts, he said. What were the facts in *Downum?* Downum was not formally arraigned in the presence of the first jury, no evidence was presented for or against him, nor was he required to make any part of a defense. Since the trial went forward within forty-eight hours, he was not subjected to additional expenses of any magnitude (if, indeed, he was paying for his own defense) or to any embarrassment. In fact, a reasonable man would surely conclude that he was not being harassed, that the prosecutor was innocent of any evil design against him, and that, therefore, it was a gross miscarriage of justice to allow this harmless technical error to set him free. Rather than to resolve *any* doubt in favor of the defendant, a reasonable person would more likely contend that in this case there was little if any doubt to resolve. A court capable of the *Downum* decision is not one that believes that the primary function of a criminal trial is to determine the guilty and bring him to justice.

Consider another example from the Warren Court era. Harrison confessed to the crime of felony murder. At the trial, in order to overcome the effect of the confessions he had made to the police during interrogation, Harrison took the stand, which he was not required to do, and his own testimony placed him at the scene of the crime. He was convicted, but the Court of Appeals held his confessions inadmissible and ordered him to be retried. At his new trial, his previous oral testimony placing him at the scene of the crime was admitted, and again he was convicted. This time the Court of Appeals affirmed. But the Supreme Court reversed, holding that his oral testimony in the first trial was inadmissible in the second. The Court acknowledged that the established rule allowed testimony in a former trial to be admitted in subsequent proceedings, but insisted that the rule did not apply here because his testimony was not really voluntary; it had been "impelled" by the necessity to counteract the confessions which were later held to be inadmissible. That is to say, he had been forced to take the stand and implicate himself, just as witnesses had once been tortured in order to extract their confessions. In each case, this is self-incrimination, which the Fifth Amendment forbids; this is compelling a person to be a witness against himself.[106] This is also going to excessive lengths to avoid authorizing punishment of a confessed murderer.

CONCLUSION

The Supreme Court is not final because it is infallible, as Justice Robert H. Jackson once said in an important criminal case;[107] it is infallible because it *is* final and because, in these criminal cases, it speaks in the name of the Constitution, the supreme law of the land. The manner in which it interprets that law determines the scope of a criminal defendant's rights and therefore affects every criminal trial in the country. Thanks to the Warren Court, a criminal trial now takes, on the average, twice as long as it did in 1960, and this does not include the time consumed in appeals. The court systems, by which I mean the number of judges, prosecutors, court reporters, bailiffs, clerks, and the courtrooms themselves, were designed with the expectation that only 10 percent of the defendants would plead not guilty and would, therefore, stand trial. But the proportion of guilty and nolo contendere pleas in the federal district courts was only 78.7 percent in 1964 and has fallen steadily since then, until in 1971, it reached 61.7 percent.[108] (And there is every reason to believe that the same thing is happening in the state courts as well.) Not surprisingly, the rate of convictions has declined proportionately. In a reference to this situation, Chief Justice Burger, shortly after his appointment, said to the American Bar Association that "if ever the law is to have a genuine deterrent effect on criminal conduct, we must make some drastic changes."[109] The only change he recommended on that occasion was the appointment of additional court personnel, but he has been instrumental in effecting others. *Downum,* for example, has not been directly overruled, but its stature as a precedent was considerably reduced in 1973 when the Court, over the objections of four holdovers from the Warren Court era, refused to uphold a claim of double jeopardy in a case where, after the jury had been impaneled and sworn but before any evidence had been presented, the trial judge discovered a defect in the indictment that could not be cured by amendment and declared a mistrial. The Court held that jeopardy had not yet attached and upheld the defendant's conviction in a subsequent trial.[110] It has consistently refused to extend (and its critics insist that it has undermined) the *Miranda* rule concerning a suspect's right to remain silent.[111] *Harris* v. *New York* involved a statement made to the police by a suspect who had not been told of his rights to counsel and to remain silent. It was, therefore, inadmissible as evidence, but, because it was trustworthy according to prevailing legal standards, the Court permitted the prosecution to use it for impeachment purposes to attack the credibility of the defendant's trial testimony.[112] Perhaps most significantly, the Burger Court has acted to cut down the number of frivolous appeals filed by both state and federal prisoners. In one federal case, the prisoner petitioned for habeas corpus two years after his conviction and asked for a free transcript of his trial, which transcript, he alleged, would show that he had not had the assistance of effective counsel. A federal statute provides for free transcripts if the trial judge certifies that the asserted claim is not frivolous. The petitioner objected to this provision, and the Court of Appeals agreed with him, but the Supreme Court reversed.[113] It is not impossible that these and other recent decisions might make it easier for the criminal courts of the country to perform their primary function.

The Supreme Court, however, has the power to do more than merely prescribe the law; because of the exalted position it has held since John Marshall's time and, as a result, the character of some of the men who have served on it, it has the power profoundly to influence what it is respectable to think about the problems that arise in the law. Marshall himself and, for more recent examples, Oliver Wendell Holmes and Louis Brandeis, occupy a place in America that in other countries no judge has ever occupied. The Warren Court had its share of such men, and, because of them, its influence in the legal fraternity and in intellectual circles generally has been great indeed. It was a compassionate Court, and among the "minorities" that benefited from its compassion were criminals. Thanks to this Court, it became not only respectable but an index of a person's humanity to hold the opinion that criminals are, as a rule, deserving of mercy, not punishment, and that, on any disputed point they, and not the agents of the law, deserve the benefit of the doubt. The consequences are reflected in the statistics reported above. Rather than fearing the law, the criminally inclined had good reason to hold it in contempt, because they had good reason to know that it would not be enforced; and a law that is not enforced will not be feared, and a law that is not feared will not deter.

The law was not enforced during the Warren years because its rules were held to be unjust, or unfair—for instance, the rule that a confession obtained after extended interrogation was not by virtue of that alone a coerced confession. So the Warren Court changed what it regarded as unjust rules. The Burger Court may be able to change those rules again, but unless it can change the opinion that underlies them, an opinion the Warren Court managed to instill among lawyers on the bench and in the schools, its rule changes will prove unavailing, if only because they will prove to be temporary. We need to be persuaded again that it is not illiberal to hold the opinion that men should have reason to "fear the laws," even the laws they give themselves. Whether this will have the desired effect on the crime and murder rates depends on factors still to be considered.

CHAPTER IV

Deterrence and the Morality of Law

THE LIMITS OF DETERRENCE

THE FIRST SENTENCE of the most recent book on the deterrence question reads as follows: "This book reflects the author's suspicion that many social scientists have dismissed the deterrence doctrine prematurely."[1] Then, in some 200 pages, the author, Jack P. Gibbs, specifies in detail what has to be done by researchers in order to restate the doctrine as a systematic and researchable theory. Only when this correctly designed research is completed, he suggests, will social science be in a position to say whether punishment deters crime. But we do not have to wait upon social science for the answers to all our questions about deterrence. We know, for example, that there are fearless men and that some of them become criminals.

Orlov [who, Dostoevsky informs us, had murdered many old people and children in cold blood] was unmistakably the case of a complete triumph over the flesh. It was evident that the man's power of control was unlimited, that he despised every sort of punishment and torture, and was afraid of nothing in the world. . . . I imagine there was no creature in the world who could have worked upon him simply by authority. . . . To my questions he answered frankly that he was only waiting to recover in order to get through the remainder of his punishment as quickly as possible, that he had been afraid beforehand that he would not survive it; "but now," he added, winking at me, "it's as good as over. I shall walk through the remainder of the blows and set off at once with the party to Nerchinsk, and on the way I'll escape. I shall certainly escape! If only my back would make haste and heal!"[2]

We can take it for granted, I think, that such men will not be deterred by the fear of punishment.

We also know that the threat of punishment will be ineffective with another type of man. The idea of deterrence assumes that men will act on the basis of their self-interest and, with the threat of punishment, can be made to see that a criminal act is not in their interest. But some men are not capable of a rational calculation of their interests and of acting accordingly.

Men like Petrov are only ruled by reason till they have some strong desire. Then there is no obstacle on earth that can hinder them. . . . I wondered sometimes how it was that a man who had murdered his officer for a blow could lie down under a flogging with such resignation. He was sometimes flogged when he was caught smuggling vodka. . . . But he lay down to be flogged, as it were with his own consent, that is, as though acknowledging that he deserved it; except for that, nothing would have induced him to lie down, he would have been killed first. I wondered at him, too, when he stole from me in spite of his unmistakable devotion. . . . It was he who stole my Bible when I asked him to carry it from one place to another. He had only a few steps to go, but he succeeded in finding a purchaser on the way, sold it, and spent the proceeds on drink. Evidently he wanted very much to drink, and anything he wanted very much he *had* to do. That is the sort of man who will murder a man for sixpence to get a bottle of vodka, though another time he would let a man pass with ten thousand pounds on him.[3]

We know that such men still exist and we ought to know that the fear of punishment, even severe punishment swiftly and inexorably imposed, will not deter them from doing what they want to do. "Do you want to prevent crimes?" Beccaria asked. "See to it that enlightenment accompanies liberty."[4] But men like Petrov are beyond the reach of even enlightened rulers because they are incapable of enlightenment. The idea of deterrence cannot be dismissed as misguided, however, simply because it is sure to fail with the Orlovs and Petrovs of this world.

How do you prevent the others, the great mass of men, from committing crimes? See to it, Beccaria said, that the laws are "clear and simple" and thereby readily understood; permit no part of the nation to oppose them; see to it "that men fear the laws and nothing else";[5] and enforce the laws with a scale of punishments "relative to the state of the nation itself." This will vary—and therefore the severity of punishment will vary— with the degree of enlightenment or, to say the same thing, the degree of civilization. A nation that has just emerged from the "savage state," or one that counts an Orlov or Petrov as a typical citizen, will require harsher punishments than those that have been "softened in the social state."[6] Commerce (or business) is a great softener.

In the commercial society, men will not be enjoined to pursue (indeed, they will be discouraged from pursuing) the "imaginary" or the sacred, in the pursuit of which their every disagreement gives rise to civil strife and wars, but they will be encouraged to pursue their material self-interests. Macaulay, that keen-eyed Englishman of the nineteenth century, was describing an aspect of this when he said that the aim of the premodern philosophy was to raise men far above their vulgar wants and was noble, whereas the aim of the modern philosophy was to supply their vulgar wants and was attainable.[7] Enlightened men, taught by Beccaria and his precursors, would build their cities with an eye to business, not with an eye to heaven, and business (and the material wealth it creates) is a condition of the promised peace. This policy would give rise to more office buildings and fewer cathedrals, multinational corporations instead of crusades. "Commerce and private property are not an end of the social contract," Beccaria said, "but they may be a means for attaining such an end."[8] Commerce, as is sometimes said, would become a substitute for morality. The end was peace, and Beccaria's purpose was to show that in the enlightened commercial society crimes would be fewer and of a less violent character and that the punishments could be proportionately milder. Torture, for example, would be unnecessary because the acts and thoughts (or "words") with which it had traditionally been associated would cease to be regarded as crimes. In time, they would cease to concern men. Men would be of a milder disposition because their passions, instead of being inflamed in one great cause or another, would be directed to commerce and the acquisition of wealth—the conditions of peace and therefore of self-preservation. Such men would be softer and less inclined to vengefulness. Instead of dreaming of revenge, modern men would take out insurance policies and get on with their work. Whatever criminal tendencies they would conceal within their breasts could be easily controlled by the threat of punishment. Deterrence would work with them. They would be liberated from the engines of the old morality, but enlightened liberty would pave the way to peace. Crime would not be a problem.

"Do you want to prevent crimes?" Beccaria asked again. "See to it that enlightenment accompanies liberty." With knowledge, men would see that what appears to be an incompatibility of their interests is more apparent than real. "Knowledge, by facilitating comparisons and by multiplying points of view, brings on a mutual modification of conflicting feelings, especially when it appears that others hold the same views and face the same difficulties."

The vigorous force of the laws, meanwhile, remains immovable, for no enlightened person can fail to approve of the clear and useful public compacts of mutual security when he compares the inconsiderable portion of useless liberty he himself has sacrificed [on leaving the state of nature] with the sum total of liberties sacrificed by other men, which, except for the laws, might have been turned against him. Any person of sensibility, glancing over a code of well-made laws and observing that he has lost only a baneful liberty to injure others, will feel constrained to bless the throne and its occupant.[9]

This is Beccaria's formulation of a teaching whose original author was Hobbes. Enlightenment would remind men of the terrors of the state of nature and of the considerable material advantages of peace, and, in this fashion, teach them the necessity to obey the sovereign's laws. It might fail with the Orlovs and Petrovs, but so did the system it replaced, and, besides, in the new commercial society there would be fewer Orlovs and Petrovs. Men would be liberated from the traditional moral authority, but an enlightened self-interest would bring peace and safety.

Would it work? Exactly 100 years later Dostoevsky ridiculed the very idea of it.

But these are all golden dreams. Oh, tell me, who was it first announced, who was it first proclaimed, that man only does nasty things because he does not know his own interests; and that if he were enlightened, if his eyes were open to his real normal interests, man would at once cease to do nasty things, would at once become good and noble because, being enlightened and understanding his real advantage, he would see his own advantage in the good and nothing else, and we all know that not one man can, consciously, act against his own interests, consequently, so to say, through necessity, he would begin doing good? Oh, the babe! Oh, the pure innocent child![10]

Why, indeed, should a person of sensibility, after "glancing over a code of well-made laws and observing that he has lost only a baneful liberty to injure others," then feel constrained "to bless the throne and its occupant"—in short, why should he obey the sovereign's laws? Beccaria's answer is that it is in his interest to do so, and not simply because it is in his interest to avoid punishment. The alternative to men's obeying the laws is the return to the state of nature wherein no man's rights are secure; and men can be taught to understand that principle. No "enlightened person" can fail to see how useful is the compact that provides "mutual security" and how necessary it is that he, and everyone else, obey the laws made possible by the compact. He will then be constrained to act with others as he wants others to act with him, not because he has been taught it as a moral duty, but because the law has so commanded him and because it is in his interest to obey the law. Traditionally men had been taught that they lived under a moral law that not only forbade them to rob and assault travelers on the road from Jerusalem to Jericho but required them to follow the example of the good Samaritan and lend assistance to anyone who had been robbed and assaulted. The familiar rule, do unto others as you would have others do unto you, summed it up. Hobbes's reformulation of this expresses the difference between traditional Christian politics, or policy, and the new natural rights politics: *"Do not do that to another, which thou wouldest not have done to thyself."*[11] Under this regime, no one is taught that he must go to the assistance of travelers on the road to Jericho; one is only taught that it will not be in his self-interest to be a thief or murderer. Beccaria, like Hobbes, was confident that this system would work.

But is it not likely that some men—some wicked men—will see immediately that their interests could best be advanced if others obey the maxim while they disobey it? Rousseau thought so, which is why he, long before Dostoevsky, objected to this Hobbesian (and soon to become Beccarian) system. He said that the wicked man would profit from the just man's probity and his own injustice. In fact, the wicked man will be delighted if everyone, except himself, obeys the law.[12] Rousseau's point was that the Golden Rule, and especially Hobbes's version of it, would not be obeyed if it were to be supported only by self-interest. While it is true that the wicked man, along with everyone who thinks about it, will want to avoid a return to the lawlessness of the state of nature, he will know that his disobedience alone will not cause such a return. The conclusion from all this is that the fear of punishment will not work with the fearless (Orlov), the irrational (Petrov), or the rational and wicked (whose names we are not likely to know).

Some proportion—and perhaps a considerable proportion—of this last group might be deterred by the threat of truly ruthless punishment summarily imposed. For example, the incidence of shoplifting would probably show a marked decline if supermarket check-out clerks were authorized summarily (perhaps with small-scale guillotines conveniently located next to their cash registers) to chop off the hands of everyone apprehended in the act of stealing from the store. That is, it would show a marked decline if the management could find check-out clerks who would inflict the penalty. Whatever may be the case in Saudi Arabia, it is not likely that such people could be found in America. We can be fairly certain that such a punishment could not be imposed among us even, or especially, after a due process trial: American juries, civilized or softened by their life in the commercial or bourgeois society, would simply refuse to convict anyone of shoplifting if the crime carried a mandatory punishment of this order of severity. It was because he saw the possibility of this that Beccaria was opposed to capital punishment.

Having begun his chapter on the death penalty by demonstrating (to his own satisfaction, at least) that the sovereign has no right to impose the sentence of death on any citizen, Beccaria immediately contradicted himself by suggesting that the issue was not whether the sovereign had a right to execute for crimes but whether there were circumstances in which it was necessary to do so, and he conceded that there were.

There are only two possible motives for believing that the death of a citizen is necessary. The first: when it is evident that even if deprived of liberty he still has connections and power such as endanger the security of the nation—when, that is, his existence can produce a dangerous revolution in the established form of government. The death of a citizen thus becomes necessary when a nation is recovering or losing its liberty or, in times of anarchy, when disorders themselves take the place of laws. But while the laws reign tranquilly, in a form of government enjoying the consent of the entire nation, well defended externally and internally by force, and by opinion, which is perhaps even more efficacious than force, where executive power is lodged with the true sovereign alone, where riches purchase pleasures and not authority, I see no necessity for destroying a citizen, except if his death were the only real way of restraining others from committing crimes; this is the second motive for believing that the death penalty may be just and necessary.[13]

Thus, he was not opposed in principle to the death penalty and saw its necessity under some circumstances; but he then went on to argue that in most circumstances it was relatively ineffective because it succeeded in making only a momentary impression on those who witnessed it. Far superior in this respect was penal servitude. It provided a "long and painful example of a man deprived of liberty, who, having become a beast of burden, recompenses with his labors the society he has offended." Other men will profit by witnessing the criminal spending "a whole lifetime . . . in servitude and pain."[14] Thus, the question of the death penalty did not turn on whether the sovereign had a right to impose it, and it was not governed by any moral considerations or by the necessity, arising out of a sense of justice, of making the punishment fit the crime; the question was one of utility. What form of punishment was most fearful and, therefore, was best calculated to effect obedience to the laws? The answer to this question turned on the sentiments of the population:

The death penalty becomes for the majority a spectacle and for some others an object of compassion mixed with disdain; these two sentiments rather than the salutary fear which the laws pretend to inspire occupy the spirits of the spectators. But in moderate and prolonged punishments the dominant sentiment is the latter, because it is the only one. The limit which the legislator ought to fix on the rigor of punishments would seem to be determined by the sentiment of compassion itself, when it begins to prevail over every other in the hearts of those who are the witnesses of punishment, inflicted for their sake rather than for the criminal's.[15]

Punishment must fit the sentiments of the law-abiding population rather than the crime. It must be rigorous enough to strike fear in the hearts of that population but not so rigorous that that population sympathizes with the criminal. It must be rigorous enough to deter but not so rigorous that the people refuse to allow it to be imposed. This principle allows us to see that, except in barbaric places, shoplifting cannot in fact be deterred by a threat to chop off the hands of those who are caught. It also allows us to see why the death penalty may be regarded as the most dreadful penalty and, at the same time, why it may not deter the crimes for which it is prescribed. Precisely because it is so dreadful, juries, their compassion aroused by the sight of the offender who faces death if convicted, may refuse to bring in verdicts of guilty in cases for which death is the mandatory punishment. Thus, to generalize, an excessively severe punishment will not serve to deter Orlov, Petrov, or anyone else, because it will not be imposed.

But there is another aspect to this subject as to which Beccaria was silent, perhaps because it is an aspect that can find no place in the deterrence theory of punishment. Whether juries will in fact refuse to bring in verdicts of guilty in such circumstances depends not merely on their view of the penalty; it depends as well on their attitude toward the crime committed by the offender. The more heinous the crime, the less likely they are to feel compassion for the offender and the more likely they are to vote for the most severe penalty permitted under the law. What this means is that in imposing punishments the people will be guided not simply, or perhaps not even at all, by considerations of what is required to strike fear in the hearts of the nonoffenders, but rather by their notions of what is deserved. The worse the crime, the heavier the penalty. This, of course, is the principle of just deserts, and among unsophisticated people there seems to be what might be described as a natural tendency to adopt it. At any rate, a jury will naturally look back at the crime rather than forward to the effect of the punishment; when looking back at the crime, it is likely to feel compassion for its victims rather than for its perpetrator. In a murder case especially (so long as murder is seen as a terrible offense), it is likely to feel compassion for the family and friends of the victim (as well as for the victim himself) and to want to assist them, even to the extent of satisfying their desire for retribution. In short, the jury that is permitted to look back at the crime is likely to become angry, both at the crime and the criminal—unless, of course, it has been taught to do otherwise. Beccaria's hope was that they could be taught to do otherwise.

It should be clear from his words on the subject that the principle of deterrence is incompatible with the principle of just deserts. This does not mean that punishments inflicted because the criminals deserve them may not serve to deter others from committing similar offenses; nor does it mean that a schedule of punishments devised in order to deter may not happen to correspond to one devised to make punishments fit the crimes. But deserved punishment is for the "sake" of the crime and not for the sake of the "witnesses," as Beccaria put it, or the nonoffenders. As such, it requires a looking back at the crime to determine what it deserves, rather than a looking forward to determine whether it will deter others. It requires calculations that cannot be made by someone who holds that the purpose of punishment is only to prevent the criminal from inflicting new injuries and "to deter others from similar acts."[16] The deterrence theorist will not recognize the victim of crimes or his anger; indeed, he calls this anger a desire for revenge, and his purpose is to offer no place in a schedule of punishments for the desire for revenge, even if it goes by the name of retribution. Compassion for the victim does not enter his calculations; the only compassion he recognizes is that likely to be felt for the criminal. He is not (at least in principle) an angry man, and his purpose is now, as it was with Beccaria, to teach the law—and the judges and juries that administer the law—not to be angry. Yet, a focus on deterrence instead of on the crime may have the paradoxical consequence of undermining deterrence, or of limiting its effectiveness, not with the Orlovs and Petrovs—they are, in a sense, beyond the reach of the law—but with the great bulk of the population who are amenable to instruction by the law. This is likely to be the consequence because the population will lose sight of the immorality of crime.

The modern purpose of punishment is not to teach men that it is immoral to commit a crime, even the crime of murder, but that it is contrary to their interests to do so. Hobbes is explicit on this point. The sovereign may kill the subject, and the subject, *whether guilty or innocent,* may, to preserve himself, kill the sovereign—or the sovereign's agents: jailer, executioner, or whoever aids them and thereby threatens his life.[17] The sovereign acts with a view to his interest and the subject acts with a view to *his* interest; neither may impute blame to the other for so doing, and each, when he perceives his self-interest to require it, may kill the other. It might be said that a subject is wrong to kill, because when he entered into the contract organizing civil society he agreed not to kill, but he agreed not to kill only because others also agreed and he calculated that this was the most efficacious way to keep himself from being killed. But if the law then decrees that he must die, he is absolved of his contractual obligation not to kill. Self-preservation is prior to, in the sense of taking precedence over, all obligations. Locke, one of the acknowledged founders of modern liberalism, put this bluntly: "Everyone, as he is bound to preserve himself and not to quit his station wilfully, so by the like reason, *when his own preservation comes not in competition,* ought he, as much as he can, to preserve the rest of mankind."[18] Not even murder is intrinsically immoral. It should be prevented, and it is the function of penal laws to prevent it by demonstrating to everyone that it is not in his interest to murder; but, quite obviously, when the sovereign shows every intention of executing a man, it is in the interest of that man to kill his guards and escape.

The question is, what is the effect of a system of law that says *only* that it is not in the interest of a man to commit a crime? Of a law that designs punishments with a view *only* to demonstrating to everyone that it is not in his interest to commit a crime? Or, once again, of a law that does not impute blame to the crime committed by a man acting in what he perceives to be his own interests? The answer is, there will be more crime because once people are no longer governed by their morals-manners, as Rousseau put it, "they will soon enough discover the secret of how to evade the laws."[19] In short, deterrence will work only if the threat of punishment is combined with the conviction that the forbidden acts are not only illegal and therefore punishable but immoral. In the absence of that conviction, the easily frightened will not break the law, but the fearless will break the law, the irrational will break the law, and all the others will break the law, and the clever ones among them will do so with impunity.

THE MORALITY OF PUNISHMENT

Hobbes recognized that the natural right of each man to preserve his own life required him to enter a civil society whose purpose was to secure and enforce peace, the condition of self-preservation. Civil peace was endangered most of all, he argued, by what he called the "seditious" doctrine according to which "every man is judge of good and evil actions," and, in the circumstances of seventeenth-century Britain, it was to be expected that he also argued that the principal source of men's "private [moral] judgments" was in the teachings of the theologians, or as he said, "the spiritual power."[20] He, therefore, became the first political philosopher forthrightly to advocate the subordination of religion,[21] or what we have come to speak of as the separation of church and state. Men had to be taught that there is no morality outside the law.

The Hobbesian-Beccarian theory of punishment rests on this proposition. "By a good law," Hobbes said, "I mean not a just law: for no law can be unjust." The law is made by the sovereign power, "and all that is done by such power, is warranted, and owned by every one of the people; and that which every man will have so, no man can say is unjust."[22] Beccaria said the same thing when he wrote that the laws, and only the laws, form "the basis of human morality";[23] and the source of the laws for both men is the "expressed or tacit compacts of men," and the consideration that leads men to enter into these compacts is self-interest defined as self-preservation. In their somewhat different ways, both Hobbes and Beccaria did their best to persuade men, when entering these compacts, not to agree to the translation of what traditionally had been understood as the moral law into the positive law that would be enforced in the new civil societies; in doing this, they originated the project of separating law and morality, as we say today.

Beccaria, for example, in another of his crime prevention proposals, advised a program of decriminalization or, to adopt another contemporary usage, getting rid of victimless crimes. He said that for "one motive that drives men to commit a real crime there are a thousand that drive them to commit those indifferent acts which are called crimes by bad laws."[24] A real crime was one that disturbed the peace by, for example, harming another person; the so-called "indifferent acts" of particular concern to him were the taking of the Lord's name in vain or the worshiping of graven images, by which I mean, of course, refusing to subscribe to what were understood to be the true articles of faith. In our own day we have seen his list grow to comprise prostitution, adultery, incest, abortion, obscenity, indecent exposure, indecent speech, and drug use, to name merely some of what are held by Beccaria's successors to be "indifferent acts." John Stuart Mill stated the principle by which the law should distinguish them from "real crimes" when he wrote in his famous *On Liberty* that "the sole end for which mankind are warranted, individually or collectively, in interfering with the liberty of action of any of their number, is self-protection." Political power—which is to say, the laws—may be used "to prevent harm to others" but not to promote what is thought to be a person's "own good, either physical or moral."[25] Whether anyone commits an act that has no victim (other than himself, of course) is a matter of indifference to the law, however immoral it might once have been considered: so far as the law is concerned, a man may indulge himself to his heart's content— provided he does not indulge himself at the expense of others. (If his daughter is willing, there is no reason for the father to deprive himself of her favors.)[26] But how do you teach a man, especially a man set free by the law, not to indulge himself at the expense of others?

The Hobbesian-Beccarian answer to this question was to use the fear of punishment; the implicit answer of the liberal states founded on principles that originated with Hobbes has been to rely on private institutions to provide the moral education that the law itself may not provide. The liberal state may not preach or teach morality, but it may (or, until recently, it did) support those private institutions that preach, teach, or somehow inculcate those decent habits needed to make liberal government possible. It was in this context that Tocqueville said that when "any religion has struck its roots deep into a democracy, beware that you do not disturb it; but watch it carefully, as the most precious bequest of aristocratic ages."[27] Liberal government must preserve what it cannot itself generate, and it must do this without jeopardizing the private realm.

I shall not repeat here what I have discussed in precise detail elsewhere; it is sufficient to point out that the necessity to preserve the moral habits of the people by supporting the institutions that inculcated them was recognized by the Founders of the United States as well as by the statesmen who followed them. The First Amendment, for example, was written in such a way that, while religious liberty was guaranteed and an official church forbidden, nondiscriminatory aid to religious institutions was permitted. Horace Mann, who gained fame as a champion of public and nonsectarian education, also insisted that the schools provide moral instruction, in fact, religious instruction, to the "extremest verge to which it can be carried without invading [the] rights of conscience." Schoolchildren were taught to read and spell with the famous readers and spellers written by the pious Reverend William McGuffey; over the course of the years from 1836 to 1920, 122 million copies of his books were sold. Obscene materials were banned as a matter of course; indeed, through at least 1932 the federal law that banned them from the mails was understood not even to raise a First Amendment problem. State laws forbade indecent speech and behavior. The laws, even federal laws, supported the monogamous family, because it was understood that the family performed an essential public service in teaching children to care for others, to respect the rights of others, and to moderate the self-interest that is embodied in the rights to secure which "governments are instituted among men." In these and numerous other ways American governments sought to preserve what they were not permitted to generate, and they did so because there was a general agreement that a free self-governing society—*especially* a free, self-governing society—depended upon citizens who were not simply self-interested men.[28] The responsibility for providing such citizens was consigned, and by liberal principles had to be consigned, to the private sector, but this private sector could depend on some support from the laws.

It was a policy whose success was problematic because of the strong possibility that this legal support would languish in time and also because there would be those who would challenge its constitutionality. These challenges have come with increasing frequency recently, and the Supreme Court has, on the whole, tended to uphold them. Prayers may not be recited under public school auspices; this prohibition also extends to the reading of Bible verses; government aid may not be extended to religious schools to the extent to which they are religious; obscene speech may be proscribed by law, but for a period of about seven years, the Court ruled that nothing was obscene, and the consequences of these decisions for the institution of marriage, and, therefore, for the family, may prove to have been decisive; profane and what was once considered very indecent speech is now considered part of that "expression" protected by the First Amendment; the states may not require schoolchildren to salute the flag, and the Court has struck down every flag-desecration statute to come before it.[29] The dubious reasoning that led to these decisions is not my concern here; what is relevant is that the burden of providing or promoting the moral or civil training we need must now be borne by other institutions. One of these is the criminal law and its administration. It must somehow teach men that, while self-indulgence is permissible, it is wrong to indulge themselves at the expense of others.

Criminology refers to this educational capacity of the criminal law as general prevention, and under this label it is associated preeminently with the name of Johannes Andenaes, a Norwegian criminal lawyer. By general prevention he means the capacity of the criminal law and its enforcement to promote obedience to law not by instilling a fear of punishment, but rather by inculcating law-abiding habits. "The idea is that punishment as a concrete expression of society's disapproval of an act helps to form and to strengthen the public's moral code and thereby creates conscious and unconscious inhibitions against committing crimes."[30] Because he regarded this function of punishment to be more significant than its capacity to instill fear, and because so little was known of the mechanisms by which it worked, if it worked at all, he called for an "empirical study of the psychology of obedience to law."[31] But the question of how punishment of criminals works to inculcate habits of law-abidingness in others is not the sort of question to which "empirical study" is particularly well adapted. Yet, it is possible that some part of that question can be answered.

In the first place, it seems clear that a system of so-called punishment, by which I mean punishment designed to rehabilitate the offender, is not likely to produce the desired result. As I pointed out at the end of Chapter II, this system has the pernicious effect of causing sympathy for the criminal. The same objection can be made to a system of punishments designed solely to deter others from committing crime; this, too, as I said earlier in this chapter, distracts our attention from the crime, and this distraction makes it altogether too easy to feel compassion for the criminal. What Andenaes wants to promote are habits of law-abidingness or habits of acting justly, and the means by which that might be done must somehow incorporate or recognize the justness of what is being done when we punish. The questions to be answered by the criminal justice system must be questions of justice, or of right and wrong, and questions of whether a particular penalty will deter or whether a particular treatment will cure are not questions of justice. As C. S. Lewis has pointed out, "there is no sense in talking about a 'just deterrent' or a 'just cure.' "[32] If punishment is to perform this educative function, then, it must be a punishment of just deserts or retribution. Still another criminal lawyer and law editor, A. L. Goodhart, stated this very well, and in doing so came closer than Andenaes to identifying the mechanism by which it works:

It must be remembered that criminal law does not function in a vac-
uum, and that it cannot ignore the human beings with whom it has to
deal. There seems to be an instinctive feeling in most ordinary men
that a person who has done an injury to others should be punished for
it. . . . It has, therefore, been pointed out that if the criminal law refuses
to recognize retributive punishment then there is a danger that people
will take the law into their own hands. A far greater danger, to my
mind, is that without a sense of retribution we may lose our sense of
wrong. Retribution in punishment is an expression of the community's
disapproval of crime, and if this retribution is not given recognition
then the disapproval may also disappear. A community which is too
ready to forgive the wrongdoer may end by condoning the crime.[33]

We have become accustomed to thinking of deterrence and
retribution as independent or unrelated theories of punishment,
but Andenaes and Goodhart (and, of course, other "old-fash-
ioned" writers whom I have not mentioned) are suggesting in
this notion of general prevention that there is a point where
they come together. We can recognize that point of convergence
by adopting a very old manner of speaking, and say that the law
works by praising as well as by blaming. The law blames when
it prescribes punishment for certain acts and when it subjects
those who commit those acts to punishment. We see that easily
enough. We tend to ignore, however, the fact that in punishing
the guilty and thereby blaming the deeds they commit, the law
praises those who do not commit those deeds. The mechanism
by which this praise is bestowed on the law-abiding takes the
form of satisfying some demand that springs from an aspect of
their souls. What is satisfied is their anger.

"Many sorrows shall be to the wicked: but he that trusteth
in the Lord, mercy shall compass him about. Be glad in the Lord,
and rejoice, ye righteous: and shout for joy, all ye that are
upright in heart!"[34] What is said in Psalms about the Lord must
also be said about the law, and as belief in divine reward and
punishment declines, it must be said more emphatically about
the law: we must trust in the law, and those who do will be
rewarded. The law must respond to the deeds of the wicked,

and the righteous must have confidence that the law will respond, and do so in an appropriate manner. It must punish the wicked because the righteous or law-abiding citizens make this demand of it. They are angered by the sight or presence of crime, and anger is not merely a selfish passion.

Roosevelt Grier, the former New York Giants defensive lineman, and the other friends of Robert Kennedy see him shot down before their eyes. They are shocked, then grief stricken, then angry; but California law cannot permit them to discharge that anger on its cause, Kennedy's assassin; they must be restrained, and the appropriate way of restraining them is to assure them that it, the law, will respond to this crime. The law must assuage that anger by satisfying it, but not, as Goodhart correctly says, simply to prevent them from taking the law into their own hands.

Consider another example. A few years ago, a seven-year-old boy was brutally murdered on the lower East Side of Manhattan. The next day, in a nearby neighborhood, a twenty-eight-year-old woman was stabbed to death in the doorway to her apartment. When the police caught the man suspected of doing it, they had a hard time protecting him from an angry crowd of local residents. A week later a thirty-one-year-old man was stabbed to death by a burglar in his apartment (one of the increasing number of felony murders), this before the eyes of his wife. The *Times* account continues as follows:

On the lower East Side, most residents seemed to agree with the police that the next time a murder suspect is identified, Tuesday's mob scene is very likely to be repeated. There is a widespread feeling that the police, the courts, the entire criminal justice system simply acts out a sort of charade, and that it is up to the community to demand that justice is done. "When the police find him, they'll just say he's a sick man and send him to a hospital for two years," said . . . a Delancey Street shopkeeper. "Then he'll be right back on the street. The only thing to do is to kill this man right away, quickly and quietly."[35]

The law must not allow that to happen, and not merely because the criminal may indeed be sick; it must provide the forms of justice in order to fulfill its educative function.

Robert Kennedy's friends were angry; that East Side mob was angry; and it is not only right that they be angry (for murder is a terrible crime), but punishment depends on it and punishment is a way of promoting justice. Without anger, or as Andenaes says in an essay written eighteen years after his original discussion of "general prevention," without moral indignation, "punishment is inflicted only reluctantly."[36] Indeed, if a society is truly indifferent to crime, punishment will not be inflicted at all. But a just society is one where everyone gets what he deserves, and the wicked deserve to be punished—they deserve "many sorrows," as the Psalmist says—and the righteous deserve to be joyous. Punishment serves both these ends: it makes the criminal unhappy and it makes the law-abiding person happy. It rewards the law-abiding by satisfying the anger he feels at the sight of crime. It rewards, and by rewarding teaches, law-abidingness.

Adam Smith said we feel cheated if a criminal should die of a fever before he is brought to justice.[37] "Cheat" is, of course, the very verb we use to describe this sort of thing, and while it is fashionable in liberal circles to deplore the usage and condemn the passion that gives rise to the sentiment, neither is reprehensible. We are deprived of something very valuable when a criminal escapes punishment, even if he does so by dying.

I think, in fact, the ordinary person tends to react in the same manner if a criminal is punished before he is convicted. Consider the case of Adolf Eichmann. As much as he was hated by the Israelis, and, for that matter, by all decent men, they would have felt cheated if, when he was run down, he had simply been gunned down. He had to be brought to justice, and that could be done only by bringing him to trial, at considerable expense and not without risk. Justice requires not only punishment, it requires the forms of justice; and the reason for this is that while the law might blame the crime by summarily punishing the criminal, it cannot praise the law-abiding without providing the solemnities of a trial. There must be a trial, and it must be attended by all the dignity, majesty, and righteousness of the law, in order to place an indelible stamp of justice on what is being done; only such a trial can fully *justify* the anger that demands punishment of the criminal. Punishment justly imposed on the criminal strengthens the habit of law-abidingness among the people.

The law praises as well as blames, or praises as it blames, and, therefore, performs an educative purpose even for a liberal society. Such a society is forbidden to teach righteousness as this is understood by any church or sect, but it may certainly use the offices of the criminal law to praise the opposite of what it may blame; that is, by recognizing the right of the people to *pay back* those who rob, assault, or murder, for example, or defraud, combine to restrain trade, file false tax returns, or conspire to obstruct justice, for other examples, it may teach the rightness of not committing these "real crimes." The trial plays a necessary role in this educative function: in addition to justifying the people's anger, it guarantees—or seeks to guarantee —that the people's anger is directed at the reprehensible act instead of the unpopular actor. This, too, is a lesson that needs to be taught.

CONCLUSION

In addition to advocating that penalties not be prescribed for "imaginary crimes" but only for "real crimes," Hobbes and Beccaria also argued that the scale of punishments be determined solely with a view to *deterring* the commission of these "real crimes." Punishment was to be utilitarian in a very narrow sense. The question to be answered was not, what punishment is appropriate to this crime, or what punishment does this criminal deserve, but rather what degree of severity will deter others from committing the same crime. The effect of this was, as I have argued above, to distract our attention from the crime and the immorality of crime, to make it easy to forget the victims of crime, and to sympathize with the criminal. Paradoxically, it also makes it more difficult for punishment to do what it set out to do—namely, to deter crimes. Only under tyrannical conditions will the fear of punishment alone serve to prevent men from committing criminal acts. Punishment will promote law-abidingness, or serve the purpose of "general prevention," only if it is seen to be deserved, and it can be seen to be deserved only by a people that is capable of moral indignation at the sight of crime.

I think the ordinary American is still capable of being morally indignant at the sight of crime and criminals, but he has derived no support for this from the intellectual community. On the contrary, the effort of criminologists, judges, "law reformers," and the so-called intellectual press has been to deprive him of this anger by making him ashamed of it. In their book, he is supposed to feel compassion for the criminal and to punish him only with the greatest reluctance—in the extreme case, to clasp him to his breast. This sentiment is not confined to America. Andenaes quotes a Norwegian judge as saying that "our grandfathers punished, and they did so with a clear conscience [and] we punish too, but we do it with a bad conscience."[38] Nor is it an accident. On the contrary, this sentiment is the consequence of penology's insistence since Beccaria's time that anger, or righteous indignation, play no role in a proper system of punishment. This, in turn, was part of a much larger project. Anger too readily becomes hatred, and hatred was seen as the cause not only of excessive punishments, but, far beyond that, of the sort of wars and civil strife that characterized so much of our history, and especially the history of Britain and Western Europe during the seventeenth century. It was with a view to preventing such wars and strife that the founders of modern political philosophy devised a politics from which the vengeful aspect of human nature was to be eliminated.

Men hated Presbyterian covenanters and tied Margaret Maclachlan and Margaret Wilson to those stakes in the tidewaters of the Solway; they hated the other political party and quartered Richard Rumbold and displayed his pieces in public. When Hobbes and, following him, Beccaria, argued that anger should play no role in punishment, they did so because they recognized only too well the terrible things that could be done by angry men when that anger is allowed to grow into hatred. Rather than attempting to tame that anger, however, they sought to eliminate it. They understood that men become angry with respect to those things for which they care, and that they hate because they care deeply or love; hence, the problem of hatred might be solved by detaching men from the objects of their love.

One of these objects was God or the church of God. Anglo-Catholics hated Scotch covenanters because of their passionate attachment to the Anglo-Catholic church of God; they may have prayed for the "whole state of Christ's Church," but they denied that the Scotch covenanters were members of Christ's Church. Hobbes's solution, which became the modern solution, was to persuade men to worry about their bodies rather than what they called their souls, in fact, to worry exclusively about their bodies because that is all they were. It was thought that men who devote themselves to preserving their bodies and leading comfortable lives are much less likely to love—and hate.

Men can also love their countries and, to the extent that they do, hate foreigners. This provides a fertile ground for wars in which glory may be won but in which bodies may be killed or maimed. But the rights of man, first discovered by Hobbes, know no national boundaries, and find their ultimate home in the League of Nations and then in the United Nations, whose job it is to preserve the peace. Love of country is to be superseded by the Universal Declaration of Human Rights.

Men can also love themselves and hate those who do not recognize their merit, which is easily transformed in their own minds into their superiority; so Hobbes taught that this pride or vanity is illusory, that all men are equally contemptible, that what all men seek is nothing but power, that their anger is simply selfish, that "the worth of a man, is as of all other things, his price,"[39] and that the Leviathan (the "King over all the children of pride") should keep them in their places by causing them to fear death more than they love glory or superiority.

Hobbes also taught men actively to seek the goods of the body, which are less likely than what are thought to be the goods of the soul to give rise to love and hate; or, at least, are less likely to do so once the problem of scarcity is solved. Then all men can share in the goods produced by an ever-expanding gross national product. His successors in this respect, John Locke and Adam Smith, showed how the scarcity problem could be solved; they showed how the gross national product (originally called *The Wealth of Nations*) could be multiplied by a factor of ten, a hundred, a thousand, or even, as Locke finally leaves it, to such an extent as to make nature's original bequest appear "almost worthless."[40] They were, as we have every reason to know, right; and they and Hobbes were essentially right as to the consequences (or, at least, as to some of the consequences) of this emphasis on the goods of the body: men who pursue their material self-interest exclusively will be less likely to be loving and hating men. (In some circles they will be dismissed contemptuously as "bourgeois.") The relations among them can be expressed contractually and measured in money. Rather than seek vengeance or fight duels for injuries suffered or insults received, such men will file suits asking for compensation for contracts breached or reputations defamed.

Peace, then, and a more comfortable and gentle condition were the intended consequences of this new dispensation, and, to the extent to which they have been achieved, we who live in this time are the beneficiaries of the founders of modern political philosophy. Unfortunately, there have been other consequences: to the extent that men cease to be loving and hating men, they also become indifferent to what we know as crime. This is why Sir James Fitzjames Stephen, more than a century after Beccaria and yet well before Andenaes and Goodhart, said, and said emphatically, that "criminals should be hated [and] the punishments inflicted on them should be so contrived as to give expression to that hatred."[41] He saw that the connection between punishment and what Andenaes calls general prevention is anger. Anger is the passion that recognizes and cares about justice. Modern penology has not understood this connection.

CHAPTER V

The Morality of Capital Punishment

ANGER is expressed or manifested on those occasions when someone has acted in a manner that is thought to be unjust, and one of its bases is the opinion that men are responsible, and should be held responsible, for what they do. Thus, anger is accompanied not only by the pain caused by him who is the object of anger, but by the pleasure arising from the expectation of exacting revenge on someone who is thought to deserve it.[1] We can become angry with an inanimate object (the door we run into and then kick in return) only by foolishly attributing responsibility to it, and we cannot do that for long, which is why we do not think of returning later to revenge ourselves on the door. For the same reason, we cannot be more than momentarily angry with an animate creature other than man; only a fool or worse would dream of taking revenge on a dog. And, finally, we tend to pity rather than to be angry with men who —because they are insane, for example—are not responsible for their acts. Anger, then, is a very human passion not only because only a human being can be angry, but also because it acknowledges the humanity of its objects: it holds them accountable for what they do. It is an expression of that element of the soul that is connected with the view that there is responsibility in the world; and in holding particular men responsible, it pays them that respect which is due them as men. Anger recognizes that only men have the capacity to be moral beings and, in so doing, acknowledges the dignity of human beings. Anger is somehow connected with justice, and it is this that modern penology has not understood; it tends, on the whole, to regard anger as merely a selfish passion.

It can, of course, be that; and if someone does not become angry with an insult or an injury suffered unjustly, we tend to think he does not think much of himself. But it need not be selfish, not in the sense of being provoked only by an injury suffered by oneself. There were many angry men in America when President Kennedy was killed; one of them—Jack Ruby —even took it upon himself to exact the punishment that, if indeed deserved, ought to have been exacted by the law. There were perhaps even angrier men when Martin Luther King was killed, for King, more than anyone else at the time, embodied a people's quest for justice; the anger—more, the "black rage" —expressed on that occasion was simply a manifestation of the great change that had occurred among black men in America, a change wrought in large part by King and his associates in the civil rights movement: the servility and fear of the past had been replaced by pride and anger, and the treatment that had formerly been accepted as a matter of course or as if it were deserved was now seen for what it was, unjust and unacceptable. King preached love but the movement he led depended on anger as well as love, and that anger was not despicable, being neither selfish nor unjustified. On the contrary, it was a reflection of what was called solidarity and may more accurately be called a profound caring for others, black for other blacks, white for blacks, and, in the world King was trying to build, American for other Americans. If men are not saddened when someone else suffers, or angry when someone else suffers unjustly, the implication is that they do not care for anyone other than themselves or that they lack some quality that befits a man. When we criticize them for this, we acknowledge that they ought to care for others. If men are not angry when a neighbor suffers at the hands of a criminal, the implication is that their moral faculties have been corrupted, that they are not good citizens.

Criminals are properly the objects of anger, and the perpetrators of terrible crimes—for example, Lee Harvey Oswald and James Earl Ray—are properly the objects of great anger. They have done more than inflict an injury on an isolated individual; they have violated the foundations of trust and friendship, the necessary elements of a moral community, the only community worth living in. A moral community, unlike a hive of bees or a hill of ants, is one whose members are expected freely to obey the laws and, unlike a tyranny, are trusted to obey the laws. The criminal has violated that trust, and in so doing has injured not merely his immediate victim but the community as such. He has called into question the very possibility of that community by suggesting that men cannot be trusted freely to respect the property, the person, and the dignity of those with whom they are associated. If, then, men are not angry when someone else is robbed, raped, or murdered, the implication is that there is no moral community because those men do not care for anyone other than themselves. Anger is an expression of that caring, and society needs men who care for each other, who share their pleasures and their pains, and do so for the sake of the others.[2] It is the passion that can cause us to act for reasons having nothing to do with selfish or mean calculation; indeed, when educated, it can become a generous passion, the passion that protects the community or country by demanding punishment for its enemies. It is the stuff from which heroes are made.

THE IMMORALITY OF ABOLITION

A moral community is not possible without anger and the moral indignation that accompanies it, which is why the most powerful attack on capital punishment was written by a man, Albert Camus, who denied the legitimacy of anger and moral indignation by denying the very possibility of a moral community in our time. The anger expressed in our world, he said, is nothing but hypocrisy. His famous novel *L'Etranger* (variously translated as *The Stranger* or *The Outsider*) is a brilliant portrayal of what he insisted is our world, a world deprived of God, as he put it.[3] It is a world we would not choose to live in and, as we shall see, one which Camus himself refused to live in. Nevertheless, the novel is a modern masterpiece, and Meursault, its antihero (for a world without anger can have no heroes), is a murderer.

Meursault appears to be a stranger or an outsider because he neither loves nor hates; nor does he understand what other people mean when they speak of love or seek to attach themselves to other human beings. His mother's death and funeral, which open the novel, leave him unmoved. Whatever he does, he does, like any other animal, out of natural necessity: he eats, but standing up and without savoring his food; he has an apartment, but only because he needs shelter of some sort (and he moves all the items necessary to his existence into one room to save the trouble of cleaning the others); he takes a woman the same way he takes a meal, and just as he must shop for his food, he is willing to marry the woman if she insists on this ceremony —in fact, as he concedes, he is willing to marry anyone whose body satisfies his body's needs. Marriage is not a serious matter, he says. Nothing is serious. The world he inhabits is differentiated by night and day, heat and cold (and he enjoys swimming when the weather is hot), but is otherwise altogether homogeneous: no nations, no classes, no beauty or ugliness, justice or injustice, war or peace. He is indifferent to human artifacts, and his life is unadorned by them: the only exception is an advertisement for a laxative which he comes upon while idly glancing through a newspaper and which he idly clips and pastes in an album. He has, willy-nilly, acquaintances among those with whom he works and dwells, but no friends; like an animal or a god he is self-sufficient: he never once frowns, smiles, or laughs. He accepts an invitation to a meal, but only to be spared the trouble of preparing his own. Utterly without imagination or ambition, he will live in Paris, if his employer sends him there, or remain in Algiers; like marriage, his place of residence makes no difference to him. He is equally indifferent to a kindness shown him or a cruelty inflicted, whether by a neighbor on a dog or by another neighbor on a mistress; in the same spirit he is willing to share in the cruelty inflicted on two men who seek to revenge a wrong committed on the sister of one of them. He ends up killing one of them, not because he hates or needs or profits or for any other human reason, but because of the sun *("à cause du soleil")*. As he later tells the examining magistrate, he does not regret the murder: rather than regretting it, he is somewhat annoyed or bored by the business *("plutôt que du regret véritable, j'éprouvais un certain ennui")*. He then says that he thinks the magistrate did not understand him.

Up to this point, Camus's is a terrible indictment brilliantly achieved, an indictment of Hobbesian man seen not in the state of nature or upon his first bursting onto the stage of history— Meursault is neither brute nor the vulgar "bourgeois gentleman" of Molière's play—but seen at the end of history, so to speak. Here he is body-preserving man deprived not only of his dreams of heaven and glory, friendship and justice, but even of his avarice; he is the man who wants nothing and, as we shall see soon enough, fears only death. One can understand why his sometime friend, Jean-Paul Sartre, likened Camus to the French moralists of the seventeenth century. Then, abruptly, Camus's perspective changes, or he makes us see what perhaps we ought to have seen all along: Meursault is an "outsider" not because he is an inhuman man in a human world, but because he is the only honest man in a world of hypocrites. He alone understands that the universe provides no support for what men in their ignorance persist in regarding as the human things, say, love and justice. And in the end Camus asks the reader (and apparently succeeds with most, which is why it is a very immoral book) to identify with that man. As he wrote in his notebook in answer to a critical review of the book, "there is no other life possible for a man deprived of God, and all men are in that position."[4]

Meursault is jailed and spends some months awaiting trial, during which time he is frequently interrogated by his lawyer and the examining magistrate. There is no question of his guilt, and he feels no remorse and refuses to pretend to any, but his lawyer wants to establish extenuating circumstances—for example, that, because of his mother's death, he had not been himself when he shot the man. What sort of man was he when he was himself? That becomes an issue in the trial and much is made of the fact that he had not shed a tear at his mother's funeral. He cannot understand why so much—indeed, why anything—is made of his behavior on that occasion. The various people he encounters in the course of his incarceration are repelled by him at first, or pretend to be, but in time he manages to get on well enough with them; he also manages to accommodate himself to his confinement. He learns to sleep sixteen to eighteen hours a day. He tells us that he had often thought that he could learn to live in the trunk of a dead tree, with nothing to do but doze and gaze at the drifting clouds—an idyll (of a sort) to be interrupted by a bit of coupling with Marie (or anyone else) on Sundays. It is only after he is convicted and is sentenced to death that he experiences, apparently for the first time in his life, hope: he hopes somehow to avoid death. To the question of why he wants to live, or what he wants to do if he lives, Meursault has no answer.

Meursault's only moment of passion comes at the end of the novel when he denounces a priest who, almost in despair, is exhorting him to acknowledge his sin and repent. He had killed a man without anger—*à cause du soleil*—but the priest he seizes by the scruff of the neck in the only fit of anger he ever displays. And what had the priest done to arouse him? He had asked him to acknowledge that life had some meaning. This from a priest who, because he was celibate, could not even be sure he was alive. *(Copulo ergo sum.)* Sadly the priest leaves the cell and Meursault becomes calm, realizing that this one burst of anger had served a purpose: it had washed him clean of his one (so-called) human quality, his selfish hope to avoid death. Now he was able to accept the truth by which he had lived: that the universe is "benignly indifferent" to how he or anyone else lives. Of course, the law is not indifferent to how he lived—for example, the law forbade him to commit murder—but the law is simply a collection of arbitrary conceits; other people were not indifferent to how he lived—for example, they expressed dismay at his lack of attachment to his mother—but other people are hypocrites.

The author of this antimorality tale was, nevertheless, one of the genuine heroes of his time, a wartime hero of the French Resistance who edited the underground anti-Nazi paper, *Combat,* and a postwar hero as well: unlike Jean-Paul Sartre, with whom he broke on the issue, Camus refused to condone Stalinism. One might say that his life was dedicated to finding a basis for the way he himself lived (and Meursault did not live). As he wrote in his notebook, "Society needs people who weep at their mothers' funerals."[5] On the occasion of their break, Sartre wrote this of him and to him:

It was in 1945: we discovered you, Camus, the Resistant, as we had already discovered Camus, the author of *L'Etranger*. And when we compared the editor of the clandestine *Combat* with that Meursault who carried his honesty to the point of refusing to say that he loved his mother and his mistress, and whom our society condemned to death, and when we knew above all that you had never ceased to be both the one and the other, this apparent contradiction helped us to understand ourselves and the world.[6]

But what was to Sartre an "apparent contradiction" was to Camus a contradiction simply, but a contradiction he tried to paper over.

He was a passionate opponent of capital punishment. He denounced it because, among other reasons, it deprived a man of the opportunity to repent and to make amends. Even Bernard Fallot, who commited horrible deeds for the Gestapo, was remediable; it was Fallot, Camus tells us, who said that his greatest regret was that he had come to know the Bible only while awaiting his execution. Had he known it earlier, he would not have been a criminal and would not have been on death row.* Poor Fallot. Poor Fallot? Meursault would have flung that Bible in the face of any priest who deigned to offer it to him, and then, cleansed of his anger, would have shrugged his shoulders.

Camus denounced capital punishment mainly because, as he saw it, "our civilization has lost the only values that, in a certain way, can justify that penalty. . . . [the existence of] a truth or a principle that is superior to man."[7] Whatever Meursault's judges thought they were doing, or whatever other unsophisticated men think they are doing when they call for the death penalty, "all thinking members of our society" know that nothing is superior to man and, therefore, that nothing can justify this terrible penalty. There is no basis for friendship and no moral law; therefore, no one, not even a murderer, can violate the terms of friendship or break that law.

If, however, the universe is "benignly indifferent" to how we live, how can it care whether we, in our naïveté, execute Fallot,

*See above p. 39.

Meursault, or anyone else for what we, in our innocence, call their immoral and illegal acts? Camus could not, in fact, adhere intransigently to this view of the world; he himself was a morally indignant man, and he knew that if there was no basis for anyone else's moral indignation, there could be no basis for his own. This is why he assiduously sought such a basis, principally in his essay on "man in revolt," which he entitled, *L'Homme Révolté,* or *The Rebel,*[8] and which was the cause of his break with Sartre and other French intellectuals who supported the Soviet Union. It is not necessary for me to judge whether Camus succeeded in this undertaking; I need only point to the answer he gave in his impassioned attack on the death penalty. There he said that the only thing that binds men together is their "solidarity against death," and a judgment of capital punishment "upsets" that solidarity.[9] The purpose of human life is to stay alive. When the abolitionists speak of the death penalty as a denial of the dignity of man, this is what they mean and— surprisingly considering their moral pretentiousness—this is all they mean.

The abolitionists are the moralists, their opponents (the "hang-hards") the immoralists; they respect human life, the others show disdain for it; they recognize man's dignity, the others are blind to every human consideration. This is what the abolitionists say, but the opposite is closer to the truth. Abe Fortas, writing after he stepped down from the Supreme Court, is merely echoing Meursault when he says that the "essential value," the value that constitutes the "basis of our civilization," is a "pervasive, unqualified respect for life."[10] This unqualified respect for life forbids us, he says, to take anyone's life, even a murderer's life. But even a moment's reflection shows that our respect for life is not and has never been "unqualified." We send men into battle knowing that some of them will lose their lives. By what right do we do this? By what right deriving from the "basis of our civilization" do we expect citizens to stand ready to give their lives for their country? Well, in fact, by the same right that led Lincoln to believe, or at least to hope, that Mrs. Bixby might be consoled by "the thanks of the Republic [her sons] died to save" or to hope that she might derive a "solemn pride" for having "laid so costly a sacrifice upon the altar of freedom." Similar considerations led the Founders in 1776 to pledge their "lives"—as well as their "fortunes" and their "sacred honor"—to the cause of our independent establishment as a nation. The men who founded this country, as well as its greatest defenders, thought that what was essential was not *that* one live but *how* one lives, Meursault and Fortas to the contrary notwithstanding.

Then Justice Brennan, still on the Court, says the death penalty does not "comport with human dignity" because it treats "members of the human race as nonhumans, as objects to be toyed with and discarded." On the contrary, it treats them as responsible moral beings. Did not Washington refuse to commute Major André's death sentence, and did not André go to his death with dignity? And was this not also true of the American spy, Nathan Hale, whose statue stands in the Yale Yard, with hands tied behind the back and head held high, presumably as an inspiration to the undergraduates who are supposed to look upon their country—"for God, for Country, and for Yale"—as something worth dying for? The legendary Hale regretted that he could die only once for it. The British did not toy with him, any more than the Americans toyed with André; in fact, by executing Hale the British provided his countrymen, then and since, with a standard against which to measure the greatness of his deeds. If we cannot say Hale achieved dignity by being put to death, we can say he achieved it by his willingness to serve his country at the risk of death, and the reality of that risk is a measure of his greatness in American eyes. By way of claiming dignity for his own position, Justice Brennan also says that the authors of the cruel and unusual clause of the Eighth Amendment intended to forbid all punishments that do not comport with human dignity, and that the death penalty

The Morality of Capital Punishment

does not comport with human dignity because it is too severe, and that it is too severe because it causes death. Of course it does. But, as Brennan knows, the authors of the Eighth Amendment were not opposed to it, and, therefore, could not have regarded it as too severe, and, therefore, could not have regarded it as incompatible with human dignity. Brennan concludes by saying that "even the vilest criminal remains a human being possessed of human dignity,"[11] which is cited as evidence of Brennan's humanism. But what sort of humanism is it that respects equally the life of Thomas Jefferson and Charles Manson, Abraham Lincoln and Adolf Eichmann, Martin Luther King and James Earl Ray? To say that these men, some great and some unspeakably vile, equally possess human dignity is to demonstrate an inability to make a moral judgment derived from or based on the idea of human dignity. Understood as Brennan understands it, the term should be dropped from the debate; it is meaningless, empty, as empty as the morality he and his abolitionist colleagues espouse.

There are vast differences between Camus, a man of deep perception and an elegance of expression, and Fortas and Brennan; but they share a single vision of the world in which we are supposed to be living. Camus, however, gave it a label appropriate to this vision: a world without dignity, without morality, and indifferent to how we live. This was the world that may not impose the sentence of death on anyone—or, for that matter, punish anyone in any manner—or ask any patriot to die for it. The question is whether we can live in such a country or in such a world.

FOR CAPITAL PUNISHMENT

THE MORAL NECESSITY OF CAPITAL PUNISHMENT

Like Meursault, Macbeth was a murderer, and like *L'Etranger*, Shakespeare's *Macbeth* is the story of a murderer; but there the similarity ends. As Lincoln said, "nothing equals Macbeth." He was comparing it with the other Shakespearian plays he knew, the plays he had "gone over perhaps as frequently as any unprofessional reader . . . Lear, Richard Third, Henry Eighth, Hamlet"; but I think he meant to say more than to imply merely that none of them equaled *Macbeth*. I think he meant that no other literary work equaled it. "It is wonderful," he said.[12] It is wonderful because, to say nothing more here, it teaches us the awesomeness of the commandment, thou shalt not kill.

Macbeth's murder of Duncan the king was no senseless or mean act; Macbeth wanted to be king and, on the basis of merit alone, deserved to be king, much more so than Duncan. Duncan was not a wise king. Although he was not witness to the alleged treachery and had to rely on the unsubstantiated word of another, he nevertheless summarily condemned the thane of Cawdor to death; he then bestowed Cawdor's title on Macbeth and went on, unnecessarily, to settle the succession to the throne on his own eldest son, even though he recognized Macbeth as the worthiest of his subjects; and, finally, he capped these acts by putting himself in Macbeth's power by agreeing to be his houseguest. Yet, however disappointed in his hopes and in spite of the opportunity the king foolishly afforded him, Macbeth held back. He respected the laws and conventions that stood between him and the throne, including those that forbade the act that would bring him to it. Duncan was not only king by grace of God ("the Lord's anointed," as Macduff referred to him); he was Macbeth's kinsman and, at the time of the murder, his guest.

... He's here in double trust:
First, as I am his kinsman and his subject,
Strong both against the deed; then as his host,
Who should against his murderer shut the door,
Not bear the knife myself.[13]

But he was driven by such a force that he had, nevertheless, to contemplate the act, even knowing that he would risk eternal damnation. He would, he said, risk "the life to come," except that Scotland, too, had laws, laws that he could ignore only at his immediate peril. "We still have judgment here," he admitted, and other men would not hesitate to enforce it if they could. Duncan's virtues may have been modest, but they were appreciated, and they would "plead like angels, trumpet-tongued" against his murderer. As a man who appreciated justice, Macbeth could not complain about that: it is a characteristic of justice to be "even-handed" and, therefore, to commend "th' ingredients of our poison'd chalice to our own lips."

Against all this was only his "vaulting ambition," and the knowledge, which Lincoln must have appreciated because he knew it of himself,* that this ambition was not vain or preten-

---

*It would take me too far afield to attempt to demonstrate that Lincoln, contrary to the legend that he himself helped to write, was the uncommonest of men; and, besides, that demonstration has already been made, and made with a clarity and wisdom that I could not hope to match. (See Harry V. Jaffa, *The Crisis of the House Divided* [Garden City, N.Y.: Doubleday, 1959], ch. 9.) I shall merely say that according to his law partner of many years, William Henry Herndon, Lincoln's ambition "was a little engine that knew no rest" and that Lincoln understood ambition, especially ambition pushed "to its utmost stretch." In one of his greatest speeches, delivered when he was not yet twenty-nine years old, he warned of the "towering genius" whose ambition could not be satisfied by a seat in Congress, or a governorship, or even the presidency. Such places, he said, were not for those who belong *"to the family of the lion, or the tribe of the eagle.* What! think you these places would satisfy an Alexander, a Caesar, or a Napoleon? Never! Towering genius disdains a beaten path. . . . It sees *no distinction* in adding story to story, upon the monuments of fame, erected to the memory of others. It *denies* that it is glory enough to serve under any chief. . . . It thirsts and burns for distinction. . . ." (Speech to the Young Men's Lyceum of Springfield, Illinois, January 27, 1838. *The Collected Works of Abraham Lincoln,* vol. 1, p. 114). Edmund Wilson was one of the few who understood that Lincoln was capable of projecting himself "into the role against which he was warning" (*Patriotic Gore: Studies in the Literature of the American Civil War* [New York:

tious. Macbeth was a great man; it was principally his valor that had saved Scotland. The king acknowledged this and, moreover, acknowledged Macbeth's claim even to the throne when, bestowing on him Cawdor's title, he did so as an "earnest of a greater honor." This could only have been the throne or the right to succeed to it. So Macbeth was contending for the place for which he was by nature suited. He sought to rule. In what other place can a man be fully a man; in what other place can he exercise all the virtues of a man? Aristotle argued this point thematically, and Winston Churchill acknowledged its truth in May 1940 when he was finally made prime minister. (Even though the world was collapsing around him, Churchill said he was conscious of a profound sense of relief: "At last I had the authority to give direction over the whole scene.")[14] It was his greatness, and more precisely, his capacity for moral greatness, that lay behind Macbeth's vaulting ambition and led him to at least consider committing the crime required of him to satisfy it; but it was even so a moral weakness that, finally, led him to act. He would, he explained, "dare do all that may become a man [and he] who dares do more is none." And what "beast" was it, asks his wife, who first proposed this enterprise to her? "When you durst do it, then you were a man." This charge of cowardice resolved him.

So he murdered: Duncan the king; then the guards whom he first accused of killing the king; then Banquo, the only man he feared (and not, but only through a mishap, Banquo's son); then Macduff's wife and children, all of them. ("All my pretty ones?/Did you say all? Oh hell-kite! All?/What, all my pretty chickens and their dam/at one fell swoop?")[15]

What can a dramatic poet tell us about murder? More, probably, than anyone else, if he is a poet worthy of our considera-

---

Oxford University Press, 1962] p. 108). But, as Jaffa demonstrates, he was also capable of projecting himself into a role "transcending that of Caesar and opposed to Caesar." At any rate, this was the Lincoln who could say of the play *Macbeth:* "It is wonderful."

tion, and yet nothing that does not inhere in the act itself. In *Macbeth,* Shakespeare shows us murders committed in a political world by a man so driven by ambition to rule that world that he becomes a tyrant. Is that a true account of a great but unbridled ambition? He shows us also the consequences, which were terrible, worse even than Macbeth feared. The cosmos rebelled, turned into chaos by his deeds. He shows a world that was not "benignly indifferent" to what we call crimes and especially to murder, a world constituted by laws divine as well as human, and Macbeth violated the most awful of those laws. Because the world was so constituted, Macbeth suffered the torments of the great and the damned, torments far beyond the "practice" of any physician.

> Will all great Neptune's ocean wash this blood
> Clean from my hand? No, this my hand will rather
> The multitudinous seas incarnadine,
> Making the green one red.[16]

He had known glory and had deserved the respect and affection of king, countrymen, army, friends, and wife; and he lost it all. At the end he was reduced to saying that life "is a tale/Told by an idiot, full of sound and fury,/Signifying nothing"; yet, in spite of the horrors provoked in us by his acts, he excites no anger in us. We pity him; even so, we understand the anger of his countrymen and the dramatic necessity of his death. *Macbeth* is a play about ambition, murder, tyranny; about horror, anger, vengeance, and, perhaps more than any other of Shakespeare's plays, justice. Because of justice, Macbeth has to die, not at his own hand—he will not "play the Roman fool, and die/On [his] own sword"—but at the hand of the avenging Macduff. The dramatic necessity of his death would appear to rest on its *moral* necessity. Is that right? Does this play conform to our sense of what a murder means? Lincoln thought it was "wonderful."

Surely we recognize that Shakespeare's is a truer account of murder then the one provided by Camus, and by truer I mean truer to our natural moral sense of what a murder is and what are the consequences that attend it. Shakespeare shows us vengeful men because there is something in the souls of men —men then and men now—that requires such crimes to be revenged. Can we imagine a world that does not take its revenge on the man who kills Macduff's wife and children? (Can we imagine the play in which Macbeth does not die?) Can we imagine a people that does not hate murderers? (Can we imagine a world where Meursault is an outsider only because he does not *pretend* to be outraged by murder?) To ask these questions is to ask whether we can imagine a world without Shakespeare's poetry, because that poetry is a reflection of the moral sense we have, and it would be impossible on the basis of the moral sense that the abolitionists insist we ought to have. The issue of the death penalty can be said to turn on whether Shakespeare's or Camus's is the more telling account of murder.

CONCLUSION

There is a sense in which punishment may be likened to dramatic poetry or the purpose of punishment to one of the intentions of a great dramatic poet (and Shakespeare is clearly the greatest in our language). The plots of Shakespeare's tragedies involve political men—Caesar the emperor, Coriolanus the general, Lear the king, Hamlet the son of a king, and others, including, of course, Macbeth who would be king—and this is not fortuitous, nor does it represent the prejudices of a poet who lived in an aristocratic age. He chose to write about such men because the moral problems can be made fully intelligible only in what they do or do not do and in the consequences of what they do or do not do. Dramatic poetry depicts men's actions because men are revealed in, or make themselves known through, their actions; and the essence of a human action consists in its being virtuous or vicious.[17] Only a ruler or a contender for rule can act with the freedom and on a scale that allows the virtuousness or viciousness of human deeds to be fully displayed. Macbeth was such a man and in his fall, brought about by his own acts, and in the consequent suffering he endured, is revealed the meaning of morality. In *Macbeth* the majesty of the moral law is demonstrated to us; as I said, it teaches us the awesomeness of the commandment, thou shalt not kill. In a similar fashion, the punishments imposed by the legal order remind us of the reign of the moral order; not only do they remind us of it, but by enforcing its prescriptions, they enhance the dignity of the legal order in the eyes of moral men, in the eyes of those decent citizens who cry out "for gods who will avenge injustice."[18] Reenforcing the moral order is especially important in a self-governing community, a community that gives laws to itself.

That the American legal order must, in the eyes of its citizens, have this dignity is the substance of Madison's argument in the Forty-ninth *Federalist.* In it he was responding to Jefferson's suggestion that there be conventions of the people whenever "any two of the three branches of government," by extraordinary majorities, shall concur in the opinion that the Constitution should be amended. Madison opposed this suggestion; he saw that these appeals, especially if they were to be frequent, would "deprive the government of that veneration which time bestows on everything, and without which perhaps the wisest and freest governments would not possess the requisite stability." Government rests on opinion, he went on, and the strength of opinion in each individual depends in part on the extent to which he supposes others to share it and in part on its venerableness. Such factors would not matter in a "nation of philosophers"; among such a people a "reverence for the laws would be inculcated by the voice of enlightened reason." But there can be no nation of philosophers, or even one governed by philosophers, and any real government, even "the most rational" government, "will not find it a superfluous advantage to have the prejudices of the community on its side."

I can illustrate Madison's point, and show its relevance to capital punishment, by saying first that if the laws were understood to be divinely inspired or, in the extreme case, divinely given, they would enjoy all the dignity that the opinions of men can attach to anything and all the dignity required to insure their being obeyed by most of the men living under them. Like Duncan in the opinion of Macduff, they would be "the Lord's anointed," and they would be obeyed even as Macduff obeyed the laws of the Scottish kingdom. Only a Macbeth would challenge them, and only a Meursault would ignore them. But the laws of the United States are not of this description; in fact, among the proposed amendments that became the Bill of Rights was one declaring, not that all power comes from God, but rather "that all power is originally vested in, and consequently derives from the people"; and this proposal was dropped only because it was thought to be redundant: the Constitution's Preamble said essentially the same thing, and what we know as the Tenth Amendment reiterated it.[19] So Madison proposed to make the Constitution venerable in the minds of the people, and Lincoln, in the Lyceum speech referred to above,* went so far as to say that a "political religion" should be made of it. They did this not because the Constitution and the laws made pursuant to it could not be supported by "enlightened reason," but because they feared enlightened reason would be in short supply; they therefore sought to augment it. The laws of the United States would be obeyed by some men because they could hear and understand "the voice of enlightened reason," and by other men because they would regard the laws with that "veneration which time bestows on everything."

But, as our history attests, this is only conditionally true. The

*See note, p. 165.

Constitution is surely regarded with veneration by us—so much so that Supreme Court justices have occasionally complained of our habit of making "constitutionality synonymous with wisdom,"[20] or wisdom synonymous with constitutionality —but the extent to which it is venerated and its authority accepted depends on the compatibility of its rules with our moral sensibilities, for the Constitution, despite its venerable character, is not the only source of these moral sensibilities. There was even a period before slavery was abolished by the Thirteenth Amendment when the Constitution was regarded by some very moral men as an abomination: William Lloyd Garrison called it "a convenant with death and an agreement with Hell," and there were honorable men holding important political offices and judicial appointments who refused to enforce the Fugitive Slave Law even though its constitutionality had been affirmed.[21] In time this opinion spread far beyond the ranks of the original Abolitionists until those who held it comprised a constitutional majority of the people, and slavery was abolished. But Lincoln knew that more than amendments were required to make the Constitution once more worthy of the veneration of moral men. This is why, in the Gettysburg Address, he made the principle of the Constitution an inheritance from "our fathers," and asked the living generation to dedicate themselves to the cause that the Gettysburg dead had left "unfinished," so that generations yet unborn might enjoy a "new birth of freedom." For the same reason, in his Second Inaugural he called upon the nation to see in the Civil War the expiation demanded by a just God for the sin of slavery. As Harry V. Jaffa has shown,[22] the Constitution had not only to be cleansed of its aspects of slavery, but, if it were once again to be an object of veneration, it would have to be exalted, its dignity enhanced. This Lincoln sought to do and this, I think, he accomplished. That it should be so esteemed is, as I said before, especially important in a self-governing nation that gives laws to itself, because it is only a short step from the principle that the laws are merely a product of one's own will to the opinion that the only consideration that informs the law is self-interest; and this opinion is only one remove from lawlessness. A nation of simply self-interested men will soon enough perish from the earth.

It was not an accident that Lincoln spoke as he did at Gettysburg or that he chose as the occasion for his words the dedication of a cemetery built on a portion of the greatest battlefield of the Civil War. Two and a half years earlier, in his First Inaugural, he had said that Americans, north and south, were not enemies but friends, and must not be enemies. Passion had strained but must not be allowed to break the bonds of affection that tied them one to another. He closed by saying this: "The mystic chords of memory, stretching from every battle-field, and patriot grave, to every living heart and hearthstone, all over this broad land, will yet swell the chorus of the Union, when again touched, as surely they will be, by the better angels of our nature." The chords of memory that would swell the chorus of the Union, when touched by a Lincoln, could be touched, even by a Lincoln, only on the most solemn of occasions, and in the life of a nation no occasion is more solemn than the burial of patriots who have died defending it on the field of battle. War is surely an evil, but as Hegel said, it is not an "absolute evil."[23] It exacts the supreme sacrifice, but precisely because of that it can call forth the sublime rhetoric of a Lincoln. His words at Gettysburg serve to remind Americans in particular of what Hegel said people in general needed to know, and could be made to know by means of war and the sacrifices demanded of them in wars, namely, that their country is something more than a "civil society" the purpose of which is simply the protection of individual and selfish interests.

Capital punishment, like Shakespeare's dramatic and Lincoln's political poetry (and it is surely that, and was understood by him to be that) serves to remind us of the majesty of the moral order that is embodied in our law and of the terrible consequences of its breach. The law must not be understood to be merely statute that we enact or repeal at our will and obey or disobey at our convenience, especially not the criminal law. Wherever law is regarded as merely statutory, men will soon enough disobey it, and they will learn how to do so without any inconvenience to themselves. The criminal law must possess a dignity far beyond that possessed by mere statutory enactment or utilitarian and self-interested calculations; the most powerful means we have to give it that dignity is to authorize it to impose the ultimate penalty. The criminal law must be made awful, by which I mean, awe-inspiring, or commanding "profound respect or reverential fear." It must remind us of the moral order by which alone we can live as *human* beings, and in our day the only punishment that can do this is capital punishment.

That was not always the case. In the beginning, banishment was considered the equal to the death penalty in severity and significance: Cain was not put to death but, instead, was banished "from the presence of the Lord" to become a "fugitive and vagabond" on the earth, unfit to live in the human community —or, as Justice Felix Frankfurter once said respecting certain American criminals, unfit "to remain in the communion of our citizens."[24] But he said that in a dissenting opinion; the Court's majority said that Americans may no longer be banished or punished by being deprived of their citizenship. They may voluntarily renounce their citizenship, but imposed as punishment, expatriation is unconstitutionally cruel and unusual.[25] Citizenship, said Chief Justice Warren, is the right to have rights, and Congress may not deprive anyone of that right, no matter what duties he shirks or what crimes he commits. Even a traitor who levies war against the United States is entitled to remain a citizen of the United States if, for some reason (perhaps because he is uncertain who is going to win that war), he wishes to do so. The essence of American citizenship, as the Warren Court saw it, consists in the right to keep one's options open, so to speak, rather like Meursault (except that Meursault would regard loss of citizenship as no punishment at all). The justices may not know it, but this understanding of the rights and duties of American citizenship owes much to Beccaria, who devoted the chapter following his chapter on the death penalty to "banishment and confiscations," and in the course of it said that the "loss of possessions is a punishment greater than that of banishment."[26]

Beccaria opposed both banishment and capital punishment because he understood that both were inconsistent with the principle of self-interest, which was the basis of the political order he favored. If a man's first or only duty is to himself, of course he will prefer his money to his country; he will also prefer his money to his brother. In fact, he will prefer his brother's money to his brother, and a people of this description, or a country that understands itself in this Beccarian manner, can put the mark of Cain on no one. For the same reason, such a country can have no legitimate reason to execute its criminals, or, indeed, to punish them in any manner. What would be accomplished by punishment in such a place? Punishment arises out of the demand for justice, and justice is demanded by angry, morally indignant men; its purpose is to satisfy that moral indignation and thereby promote the law-abidingness which, it is assumed, accompanies it. But the principle of self-interest denies the moral basis of that indignation.

Not only will a country based solely on self-interest have no legitimate reason to punish; it may have no need to punish. It may be able to solve what we call the crime problem by substituting a law of contracts for a law of crimes. According to Beccaria and Hobbes's social contract, men agree to yield their natural freedom to the "sovereign" in exchange for his promise to keep the peace. As it becomes more difficult for the sovereign to fulfill his part of the contract, there is a demand that he be made to pay for his nonperformance. From this come compensation or insurance schemes embodied in statutes whereby the sovereign (or state), being unable to keep the peace by punishing criminals, agrees to compensate its contractual partners for injuries suffered at the hands of criminals, injuries the police are unable to prevent. The insurance policy takes the place of law enforcement and the *posse comitatus,* and John Wayne and Gary Cooper give way to Mutual of Omaha. There is no anger in this kind of law and none (or no reason for any) in the society. The principle can be carried further still. If we ignore the victim (and nothing we do can restore his life anyway), there would appear to be no reason why—the worth of a man being his price, as Hobbes put it—coverage should not be extended to the losses incurred in a murder. If we ignore the victim's sensibilities (and what are they but absurd vanities?), there would appear to be no reason why—the worth of a woman being *her* price—coverage should not be extended to the losses incurred in a rape. Other examples will, no doubt, suggest themselves.

This might appear to be an almost perfect solution to what we persist in calling the crime problem, achieved without risking the terrible things sometimes done by an angry people. A people that is not angry with "criminals" will not be able to deter crime, but a people fully covered by insurance has no need to deter crime: they will be insured against all the losses they can, in principle, suffer. What is now called crime can be expected to increase in volume, of course, and this will cause an increase in the premiums paid, directly or in the form of taxes; but it will no longer be necessary to apprehend, try, and punish criminals, which is now costing Americans more than $1.5 billion a month (a cost that is increasing at an annual rate of about 15 percent),[27] and one can buy a lot of insurance for $1.5 billion a month. There is this difficulty: as Rousseau put it, to exclude anger from the human community is to concentrate all the passions in a "self-interest of the meanest sort,"[28] and such a place would not be fit for human habitation.

When, in 1976, the Supreme Court declared death to be a constitutional penalty, it decided that the United States was not that sort of country; most of us, I think, can appreciate that judgment. We want to live among people who do not value their possessions more than their citizenship, who do not think exclusively or even primarily of their own rights, people whom we can depend on even as they exercise their rights, and whom we can trust, which is to say, people who, even in the absence of a policeman, will not assault our bodies or steal our possessions, and might even come to our assistance when we need it, and who stand ready, when the occasion demands it, to risk their lives in the defense of their country. If we are of the opinion that the United States may rightly ask of its citizens this awful sacrifice, then we are also of the opinion that it may rightly impose the most awful penalty; if it may rightly honor its heroes, it may rightly execute the worst of its criminals. By doing so, it will remind its citizens that it is a country worthy of heroes.

CHAPTER VI

Not Cruel but Unusual: The Administration of the Death Penalty

THE OPPONENTS of capital punishment had good reason to believe they would win their case in the Supreme Court. They had come close in 1972 when the Court held that the death penalty had been administered in so discriminatory, capricious, or arbitrary a manner as to be a cruel and unusual punishment, and two members of the five-man majority in those cases regarded the death penalty as unconstitutional no matter how administered. It is true that public and legislative opinion seemed to be moving against them, but if Arthur Koestler's characterization of the public support of the death penalty is accurate—that it is based on "ignorance, traditional prejudice and repressed cruelty"[1]—then it was likely that the penalty would continue to be imposed discriminatorily, capriciously, or arbitrarily, and that a majority of the Court would, sooner or later, come to the conclusion that it could be imposed in no other manner. This may yet happen. In 1976, however, seven members of the Court not only voted to uphold the death penalty statutes of three states and the sentences imposed under them, but, in the course of doing so, gave the sanction of the Constitution to the principle that criminals should be paid back for their crimes.[2]

It was this sanctioning of the retributive principle that especially disturbed Justice Marshall, one of the two dissenters. He would apparently be willing to allow executions if it could be shown that they serve some useful purpose—for example, that they serve to deter others from committing capital crimes (and he was not persuaded by Ehrlich's study suggesting that they do deter)—but to execute someone simply because society thinks he deserves to be executed is, he said, to deny him his "dignity and worth."[3] Why it would not deprive a man of his dignity and worth to use him (by executing him) in order to influence the behavior of other men, Marshall did not say; apparently he would be willing to accept society's calculations but not its moral judgments. Be that as it may, it cannot be denied that he and other abolitionists have a point: to say that someone deserves to be executed is to make a godlike judgment with no assurance that it can be made with anything resembling godlike perspicacity. In the extreme case, and some abolitionists make much of its possibility, society may execute an innocent person, and no one can assure us that this has never happened or that it will never happen in the future. Yet Bedau, probably the best known of America's abolitionists, refuses to credit it, or to rely on it as part of his case against the death penalty. He calls it "false sentimentality to argue that the death penalty ought to be abolished because of the abstract possibility that an innocent person might be executed, when the record fails to disclose that such cases occur."[4] The more likely mistakes are of a different order of magnitude.

A recent study of the manner in which homicide was punished in Philadelphia in the year 1970 discloses great and apparently unjustifiable variations in the sentences handed down, the problem being not that the sentences are too lenient or too severe, but that they are both; as the authors say, "the going price of criminal homicide is two years or twenty."[5] It was the apparently equally arbitrary imposition of the death penalty that the Court in 1972 found to be cruel and unusual, and that the statutes enacted after 1972—the so-called post-*Furman* statutes—were designed to prevent. The editors of the *Harvard Law Review*, in a careful review of these statutes, concluded that, if the 1972 decisions dictate strict limits on both sentencing and nonsentencing discretion in capital cases, none of the new laws is constitutional because none of them "fulfills these demands."[6] Juries would, they argued, easily find ways of avoiding those limits when they impose sentences, prosecutors would continue to make their own judgments as to who should be prosecuted for what, and governors would continue to commute or not to commute death sentences in an arbitrary manner. Charles Black goes so far as to insist that "caprice and mistake" are inevitable in capital cases, and that, however carefully written and whatever the language employed to force juries to follow statutory standards, no statute can prevent mistakes or reduce their incidence and magnitude to a point where they might be tolerated.[7] Nevertheless, justice requires that juries be allowed to exercise discretion.

Not all murderers deserve to be executed; not even all first-degree murderers deserve to be executed, because not all first-degree murders are equally terrible. Yet, in reaction to the 1972 Supreme Court decisions, a number of states, determined to demonstrate that they could eliminate the injustice of arbitrary capital sentencing, enacted new statutes making death the mandatory sentence for persons convicted of first-degree murder. This is a mistake, and I think most of us know it. We can recognize the difference between the culpability of Jack Ruby, for example, the killer of Lee Harvey Oswald, and that of Lee Harvey Oswald himself (assuming, of course, that he was indeed the killer of President Kennedy); we could accept a prison term, perhaps even a relatively brief prison term, for Ruby because we could accept the prospect of his return to our community; but I doubt that we could accept the same sentence for Oswald or the prospect of *his* return to our community, even if he promised never again to assassinate a president. Black, with reference to the new Georgia statute which directs the jury to decide whether the charged offense was "outrageously or wantonly vile," insists that it is "impossible to imagine a murder" that cannot be so described,[8] but surely this exaggerates; the typical jury is not that obtuse. Consider the recent case of Hamaas Abdul Khaalis and his Hanafi Muslim sect who in March 1977 seized hostages in the course of occupying three Washington, D.C., buildings and at this time stand charged with the murder of a reporter who was in one of them. The seizures were surely outrageous, irrational, and admixed with an element of bigotry; but they were provoked by a terrible event, the killing of Khaalis's children and grandchild. Five Black Muslims shot and killed two of the children, drowned three others in a bathtub, and, with its mother forced to look on, drowned a ten-day-old baby in a sink. That is an outrageous, wanton, and vile crime. Khaalis is reported as saying, "I'm waiting to see what my country is going to do about the gang in Chicago that killed my family."[9] What his country did —this being during the period when capital punishment was in ill-repute—was to sentence the five killers to life imprisonment, which Khaalis, not unreasonably, regarded as wholly inadequate. But what of the killing of Maurice Williams, the reporter who had the misfortune to be in one of the buildings during its occupation by the Khaalis group? A grave offense, surely, and one that deserves to be severely punished; but it does not deserve to be classed with the murders of the Khaalis children, and, unlike Black, I think the typical jury would agree.* When it is informed that the term "outrageously or wantonly vile" is

---

*In the event, Khaalis was sentenced to 41 to 123 years imprisonment, and Abdul Muzikir, who shot Williams, the reporter, to 77 years to life. See *New York Times*, Sept. 7, 1977, p. 18.

intended to differentiate among murders—all murders being grave offenses—a jury is capable of seeing the difference. Of course jury discretion should be limited, which is to say that statutes should provide standards to guide sentencing decisions, but it is unjust to deprive juries of all discretion. The jury is expected to exercise the community's moral judgment in a particular case involving a particular crime and a particular criminal, and no statutory language is capable of describing these particularities in advance. Besides, mandatory statutes do not in practice eliminate jury discretion: when juries are of the opinion that an offender does not deserve death, they simply do not convict him of the capital offense. It was to be expected, therefore, that the Supreme Court would, as it did, strike down the North Carolina and Louisiana statutes making death the mandatory sentence for first-degree murder.[10]

The three statutes upheld on that same day in 1976 permit jury discretion but attempt to prevent its abuse, or, to speak more reasonably, attempt to reduce the possibility of this abuse to a tolerable minimum. It remains to be seen whether, contrary to the expectations of Charles Black and the editors of the *Harvard Law Review,* they will succeed in doing so. Carefully drafted, all three statutes, especially the one from Georgia, embody procedures intended to impress on judges and juries the gravity of the judgment they are asked to make in capital cases —for example, all three require the sentencing decision to be separated from the decision respecting guilt or innocence; and in one way or another, all three imply that the death sentence is not to be looked upon as ordinary. Thus, the Georgia law requires (except in cases of treason and aircraft hijacking) a finding beyond a reasonable doubt of the presence of at least one of the aggravating circumstances specified in the statute, and requires the judge or, as the case might be, the jury to specify the circumstance found. Texas requires the jury, during the sentencing proceeding, to answer affirmatively three questions: whether the evidence established beyond a reasonable doubt that the murder was committed deliberately, whether the evidence established beyond a reasonable doubt that there was a probability that the defendant would commit criminal acts of violence in the future, and, when relevant, whether the defendant's conduct was an unreasonable response to any provocation by the deceased. The Florida statute requires a weighing of aggravating and mitigating circumstances, which are listed in the statute. Finally, all three statutes permit or require an expedited appeal to or review by their respective supreme courts, which are authorized to set aside a death sentence in order to ensure, for example, that similar results are reached in similar cases. (That this review is not perfunctory is indicated in the fact that the Florida supreme court had, at the time of the U.S. Supreme Court decisions, vacated eight of the twenty-one sentences to come before it under the new law.)[11]

These statutes are surely improvements over the ones they replaced, but in one respect they do not, in my opinion, go far enough. The very awesomeness of condemning a man to death requires the punishment to be reserved for extraordinarily heinous crimes, but throughout most of modern history this has not been the case. The historical record is sprinkled with statements to the effect that no man's property will be safe unless death is the penalty for stealing it, even if the property is no more than that which is carried casually in a pocket and the theft is accomplished merely by picking that pocket. But retributive justice requires punishment to fit the crime, which requires a schedule of punishments, ranging from the most lenient through various degrees of severity to the most awful, death, because the moral sentiments of a just people recognize that crimes range from the most petty through various degrees of gravity to the most awful, which, as we understand these things, is the taking of a human life. The law cannot reinforce these moral sentiments (and its purpose is to do just that) if it executes the pickpocket or the shoplifter as well as the murderer; to do that is to equate petty theft with murder, and petty amounts of property with a human life, and to do that *is* to deny human dignity. The law that does it will lose, and will deserve to lose, the respect it must enjoy among the people, who will neither obey it nor, when serving on juries, enforce it. To reinforce the moral sentiments of a people, the criminal law must be made awful or awesome, and, as I argued in the preceding chapter, the only way within our means to do that today is to impose the death sentence; but an execution cannot be awesome if it is associated with petty affairs or becomes a customary, familiar event. Thus, while the death penalty should not be seen as cruel, by the same token it should be seen as unusual, not in the techniques employed when carrying it out, but in the frequency with which it is carried out. It is this principle that should be embodied in statutes and impressed upon judge and jury; a properly drawn statute will allow the death penalty only for the most awful crimes: treason, some murders, and some particularly vile rapes.[12] It is not beyond the skill of legislators to draft such a statute—for example, it could provide that the death sentence be imposed *only* for "outrageously or wantonly vile" offenses—one that defers to the jury's judgment in particular cases but, at the same time, impresses upon the jury the awesome character of the judgment it is asked to make. This is not incompatible with retributive sentencing; on the contrary, retribution, unlike deterrence, precisely because it derives from moral sensibilities, recognizes the justice of mercy, the injustice of punishing the irresponsible, and limits to the severity of punishment. (If the only purpose of punishment is deterrence, why not boil murderers in oil or chop off the hands of shoplifters?) It is also compatible with the purpose of capital punishment; only a relatively few executions are required to enhance the dignity of the criminal law, and that number is considerably smaller than the number of murderers and rapists. The other purpose of punishment can be more fully accomplished by a more rigorous enforcement of the other criminal statutes.

These considerations lead me to agree with the judgments

(but not with the Court's opinions) in the most recent death penalty cases, decided July 3, 1978.[13] The two defendants in these cases had participated in the crimes leading to the death of the victims, but neither had been the "triggerpersons"; they were, nevertheless, convicted of aggravated murder. The Ohio statute provided that, upon conviction of this offense and in the absence of at least one of the three specified mitigating circumstances, the death sentence must be imposed, and it was imposed in each case. The Court reversed these judgments, but not, as was urged by Mr. Justice White in a separate opinion, because it is indeed cruel and unusual—and therefore unconstitutional—to impose a death sentence without a finding of intent to cause the death of the victim; to have based its holdings on this ground would have been altogether reasonable. What the Court did, instead, was to hold the statute unconstitutional because it limited the range of mitigating circumstances that may be considered when imposing sentence.[14] Thus, having begun in 1972 in *Furman* v. *Georgia* by complaining of the capriciousness of the sentences imposed in capital cases and suggesting that to prevent this capriciousness statutes must limit the discretion available to judges or juries when imposing sentences, the Court (albeit by a mere plurality of its members) has now begun to complain of, in effect, the absence of discretion. As a result, we are likely to see more of what the Court calls "capriciousness." As Mr. Justice Rehnquist said in dissent, "the new constitutional doctrine will not eliminate arbitrariness or freakishness in the imposition of sentences, but will codify and institutionalize it."[15] What seems plain is that the governing plurality of the Court lacks the courage of its constitutional convictions, for, although conceding the constitutionality of the death penalty, it is unwilling to allow it to be imposed on anyone who, unlike Gary Gilmore, brings an appeal. Or can it be said that the material but unacknowledged fact in these cases was that the defendants were black?

Justice Douglas voted to vacate the sentences in the 1972

cases because it appeared obvious to him that death sentences have traditionally been imposed and carried out disproportionately "on the poor, the Negro, and the members of unpopular groups."[16] There is surely some truth in this, and the chief justice acknowledged it in his dissent in 1972 when he said that "statistics suggest, at least as a historical matter, that Negroes have been sentenced to death with greater frequency than whites in several states, particularly for the crime of interracial rape."[17] That, of course, is one reason why the Court has insisted that Negroes no longer be systematically excluded from jury service; and that is also why, in its new statute, Georgia authorized its supreme court to set aside any death sentence that appeared to be the result of passion or prejudice on the part of trial judge or jury. This provision could prove to be an indication of an important change where it is most needed, because, in the period from 1930 through 1974, Georgia executed 366 of the 3,859 persons executed in the entire country, more than any other state, and of the Georgia total, 298 were blacks.[18] In themselves these statistics indicate only that the number of blacks executed is disproportionate to the number of blacks in the population and not necessarily to the number of crimes committed by blacks; but from other sources we know that this record cannot be explained by anything except the white prejudice that prevailed in that state at that time. It is too soon to draw conclusions, but it may be significant that while there were twenty persons under sentence of death in Georgia at the end of 1974, thirteen of them were white and only seven black.[19]

A recent study, however, suggests that there has been no improvement in this aspect of the racial problem. Comparing the racial composition of persons sentenced to death immediately before and after the Supreme Court decisions of 1972, Marc Riedel found that the proportion of nonwhites sentenced to death has declined in the South but has increased (from 52 percent to 63 percent of the total) in the country as a whole.[20]

He concludes from this that the new statutes have not prevented the discriminatory and "disproportionate death sentencing of non-whites", which, if true, would justify his statement that "the death penalty [even] as presently administered is unconstitutional" under the role of the 1972 decisions.[21] It may not, however, be true. The number of nonwhites sentenced to death is certainly disproportionate to their number in the population, and he says this disproportion cannot be accounted for by the "overrepresentation of non-whites among the criminal population." But this statement is tendentious. The study he cites in its support (and of which he is himself coauthor) deals exclusively with the period prior to 1972,[22] and in the study at hand which does deal with the period since 1972, he makes no attempt to investigate the question of discrimination in capital sentencing. He may be right, but on the basis of the evidence he presents, there is no way of knowing whether he is right.[23]

It is simply an unhappy fact that blacks commit a disproportionate number of the known crimes in the United States, including capital crimes. In 1974, a typical year, 57 percent of the persons arrested for murder were black; but, what is sometimes forgotten, 50 percent of homicide victims were also black,[24] and most black people, like most white people, are not criminals. What distinguishes them is that the law-abiding black population supplies a disproportionate number of the victims of crime; and it would be a cruel victory indeed if, having struggled so long and so hard, and, finally, so successfully against all the forms of injustice imposed on them by the white population, they were now to be exposed to what may be—in part, at least —preventable black crime because of the reluctance of white liberals to allow black criminals to be punished as they deserve to be punished. A country that does not punish its grave offenses severely thereby indicates that it does not regard them as grave offenses; and a country that does not punish severely its black murderers thereby indicates that it does not regard murder to be a grave offense when it is committed in the black community. This is what it would amount to, as the annual statistics on the proportion of black murder victims imply. Of course, the situation as it has existed historically in the United States can scarcely be described as one reflecting a reluctance to execute black men—on the contrary—and the future of capital punishment in America will probably depend on whether it can be imposed without regard to race and class, on white as well as black, or rich as well as poor. To execute black murderers or poor murderers because they are murderers is not unjust; to execute them because they are black or poor is unconscionable and unconstitutional. That much was decided in 1972.

There is, finally, the question of whether executions should be public. I have made much of the point that the anger that gives rise to the demand that criminals be paid back is not in principle selfish or otherwise reprehensible, and that it is a function of the law to tame that anger by satisfying and thereby justifying it. This it does when it punishes criminals; punishment, I have argued, serves to praise and reward law-abiding-ness even as it blames crime. But that anger has also to be tamed in the sense of being moderated. A proper criminal trial achieves this to some extent by forcing the jury to determine beyond a reasonable doubt that the accused is guilty as charged. In order further to calm or moderate that anger, and to impress upon the population the awesomeness of the moral order and the awful consequences of its breach, I think it necessary that executions be public. There are obvious objections to public executions, even when they are not the sort of spectacle Mandeville was describing in the eighteenth century.* No ordinary citizen can be required to witness them, and it would be better if some people not be permitted to witness them—children, for example, and the sort of person who would, if permitted, happily join a lynch mob. Executions should not be tele-

*See above, p. 24.

vized, both because of the unrestricted character of the television audience and the tendency of television to make a vulgar spectacle of the most dignified event. Yet executions must be witnessed, and witnessed by the public, which means not hidden from the view of all but prison personnel and a few others. The solution to this problem is to be found where the framers of the Constitution found part of the solution to the problem of democracy, namely, in the principle of representation. In addition to prison personnel and the others now attending them, executions should be witnessed by representatives of the people. Since the process of selecting them could not be controlled sufficiently to ensure that decorum attend every aspect of this ceremony (and I use that word advisedly), the representatives should not be specially selected for this purpose but should be those, or a part of those, already elected to the legislatures. They represent the people when they enact the statutes permitting the penalty of death, and they can represent the people when they witness its carrying out. As Madison said in the tenth *Federalist,* they are a "chosen body of citizens" who can be expected to "refine and enlarge the public views," and we have a right to expect them also to represent the public's moral indignation. If they cannot do this, they are not justified in enacting death penalty statutes. The abolitionists make this point and they are right. But executions solemnly witnessed and carried out are not barbaric; on the contrary, they enhance the awesome dignity of the law and of the moral order it serves and protects.

When abolitionists speak of the barbarity of capital punishment and when Supreme Court justices denounce expatriation in almost identical language, they ought to be reminded that men whose moral sensitivity they would not question have supported both punishments. Lincoln, for example, albeit with a befitting reluctance, authorized the execution of 267 persons during his presidency,[25] and ordered the "Copperhead" Clement L. Vallandigham banished; and it was Shakespeare's sensitivity to the moral issue that required him to have Macbeth killed. They should also be given some pause by the knowledge that the man who originated the opposition to both capital and exilic punishment, Cesare Beccaria, was a man who argued that there is no morality outside the positive law and that it is reasonable to love one's property more than one's country. There is nothing exalted in these opinions, and there is nothing exalted in the versions of them that appear in today's judicial opinions. Capital punishment was said by Justice Brennan to be a denial of human dignity, but in order to reach this conclusion he had to reduce human dignity to the point where it became something possessed by "the vilest criminal." Expatriation is said by the Court to be unconstitutional because it deprives a man of his right to have rights, which *is* his citizenship, and no one, no matter what he does, can be dispossessed of the right to have rights. (Why not a right to the right to have rights?) Any notion of what Justice Frankfurter in dissent referred to as "the communion of our citizens," of a community that can be violated by murderers or traitors, is wholly absent from these opinions; so too is any notion that it is one function of the law to protect that community.

But, contrary to abolitionist hopes and expectations, the Court did not invalidate the death penalty. It upheld it. It upheld it on retributive grounds. In doing so, it recognized, at least implicitly, that the American people are entitled *as a people* to demand that criminals be paid back, and that the worst of them be made to pay back with their lives. In doing this, it gave them the means by which they might strengthen the law that makes them a people, and not a mere aggregation of selfish individuals.

NOTES

INTRODUCTION

1. Furman v. Georgia, 408 U.S. 238, 375 (1972). Dissenting opinion.
2. Ibid., at 405. Dissenting opinion.
3. Roe v. Wade, 410 U.S. 113 (1973).
4. Weems v. United States, 217 U.S. 349, 378 (1915).
5. Trop v. Dulles, 356 U.S. 86, 101 (1958).
6. Gregg v. Georgia, 96 S.Ct. 2909 (1976).
7. Albert Camus, "Reflections on the Guillotine," in *Resistance, Rebellion, and Death,* trans. Justin O'Brien (New York: Knopf, 1961), p. 220.
8. Simon Wiesenthal, *The Murderers among Us,* ed. and with an introductory profile by Joseph Wechsberg (New York: McGraw-Hill, 1967), p. 178.
9. Furman v. Georgia, at 344, 345.

CHAPTER I

1. Gen. 4:15–16.
2. Gen. 6:9.
3. Gen. 9:5–6.
4. Exod. 20:13.
5. Lev. 24:17.
6. Num. 35:31.
7. *The Code of Maimonides* [Mishneh Torah] (New Haven, Conn.: Yale University Press, 1949), book 14 (The Books of Judges), pp. 150–51, 163.
8. Israel J. Kazis, "Judaism and the Death Penalty," in Hugo Adam Bedau, ed., *The Death Penalty in America* (Garden City, N.Y.: Doubleday, 1967), p. 172.
9. Matt. 5:17.
10. Matt. 5:21.
11. Matt. 22:37–39.
12. Charles S. Milligan, "A Protestant's View of the Death Penalty," in Bedau, *Death Penalty in America,* pp. 177–78, 180.
13. Sir Ernest Gowers, *A Life for a Life? The Problem of Capital Punishment* (London: Chatto & Windus, 1956), pp. 46, 48.

14. Matt. 18:6–7.

15. Thomas Babington Macaulay, *History of England* (Leipzig: Bernh. Tauchnitz, 1849), vol. 2, chap. 4.

16. Ibid. See also Jefferson to Roger C. Weightman, June 24, 1826, *Writings of Thomas Jefferson,* ed. Paul L. Ford, 12 vols. ["Federal" ed.] (New York: Putnam, 1904–05), vol. 12, p. 477.

17. Macaulay, *History of England,* vol. 5, chap. 15.

18. Cesare Beccaria, *On Crimes and Punishments,* trans. Henry Paolucci (Indianapolis: Bobbs-Merrill, Library of Liberal Arts, 1963), p. 5.

19. Ibid.

20. Ibid., p. 41.

21. Ibid., pp. 78, 67, 88, 81, 84, 86, 94.

22. Ibid., p. 11.

23. Thomas Hobbes, *Leviathan* (London, 1651), pt. 2, ch. 21. "And therefore it may, and doth often happen in commonwealths, that a subject may be put to death, by the command of the sovereign power."

24. Beccaria, *On Crimes and Punishments,* p. 45.

25. Immanuel Kant, *The Metaphysical Elements of Justice,* trans. John Ladd (Indianapolis: Bobbs-Merrill, Library of Liberal Arts, 1965), pp. 104–5.

26. Strauss, *Natural Right and History,* p. 197.

27. Hobbes, *Leviathan,* pt. 2, chap. 21.

28. Strauss, *Natural Right and History,* p. 197.

29. John Locke, *Second Treatise of Civil Government,* Chap. 1.

30. Jean-Jacques Rousseau, *The Social Contract,* book 2, chap. 5. See also book 4, chap. 8.

31. Baron de Montesquieu, *The Spirit of the Laws,* book 6, chap. 2. See also book 11, chap. 6.

32. Mill's views on the death penalty are contained in a speech delivered in the House of Commons on April 21, 1868. *Parliamentary Debates* (House of Commons), 3rd series, vol. 191 (London: Cornelius Buck, 1868), columns 1047–55.

33. Bentham wavered on the issue, finally coming out in opposition. See Jeremy Bentham, "The Rationale of Punishment," *The Works of Jeremy Bentham,* ed. John Bowring (London, 1843), vol. 1, pp. 525–32.

34. Thorsten Sellin, *The Death Penalty,* a report for the Model Penal Code Project of the American Law Institute (Philadelphia: American Law Institute, 1959), p. 15.

35. Bernard Mandeville, *An Enquiry into the Causes of the Frequent Executions at Tyburn* (London, 1725), p. 20.

36. Beccaria, *On Crimes and Punishments,* p. 50.

37. Albert Camus, "Reflections on the Guillotine," in *Resistance, Rebellion, and Death,* trans. Justin O'Brien (New York: Knopf, 1961), p. 177.

38. Ibid., p. 182.

39. Arthur Koestler, *Reflections on Hanging* (London: Gollancz, 1956), p. 164.

40. Michael Meltsner, *Cruel and Unusual: The Supreme Court and Capital Punishment* (New York: Morrow, 1974), p. 181.

41. Koestler, *Reflections on Hanging,* pp. 7–8.

42. O'Neil v. Vermont, 144 U.S. 323, 339 (1892).

43. Furman v. Georgia, 408 U.S. 238, 272–73 (1972).

44. See, for example, Meltsner, *Cruel and Unusual,* p. 181.

45. Hugo Adam Bedau, Foreword, in William J. Bowers, *Executions in America* (Lexington, Mass.: Heath, 1974), p. xx.

46. Beccaria, *On Crimes and Punishments*, p. 42.

47. William Bailey, "Murder and the Death Penalty," *Journal of Criminal Law and Criminology* 65 (September 1974): 416.

48. Sellin, *Death Penalty*, p. 63. His conclusions have been stated in a more guarded fashion elsewhere.

49. Hugo Adam Bedau, "Deterrence and the Death Penalty: A Reconsideration," *Journal of Criminal Law, Criminology, and Police Science* 61 (1970): 546–47.

50. Victor Gollancz, *Capital Punishment: The Heart of the Matter* (London: Gollancz, 1955), p. 7. Italics in original.

51. Gregg v. Georgia, 96 S.Ct. 2909 (1976).

52. An Act for the Punishment of Certain Crimes against the United States, 1 *Statutes-at-Large* 112 (April 30, 1790).

53. Thomas Jefferson, "Outline of a Bill for Proportioning Crimes and Punishment," *The Papers of Thomas Jefferson*, ed. Julian P. Boyd (Princeton, N.J.: Princeton University Press, 1950–), vol. 2, pp. 663–64.

54. Weems v. United States, 217 U.S. 349 (1910).

55. Trop v. Dulles, 356 U.S. 44 (1958).

56. Arthur J. Goldberg and Alan M. Dershowitz, "Declaring the Death Penalty Unconstitutional," *Harvard Law Review* 83 (June 1970): 1787–88.

57. Koestler, *Reflections on Hanging*, p. 27 and passim.

58. See the account provided by Sir James Fitzjames Stephen, *A History of the Criminal Law of England* (London, 1883; New York: Burt Franklin, n.d.), vol. 1, pp. 458–78.

59. Furman v. Georgia, 408 U.S. 238, 251–52 (1972).

60. U.S. Department of Justice, Law Enforcement Assistance Administration, National Criminal Justice Information and Statistics Service, *Sourcebook of Criminal Justice Statistics*, 1974 (Washington, D.C.: U.S. Government Printing Office, 1975), p. 516.

61. Bowers, *Executions in America*, p. 165.

62. Furman v. Georgia, at 300.

63. Various Gallup polls, conducted in 1936, 1966, 1969, and 1972, show support for capital punishment by 62, 42, 51, and 57 percent of the American people. A Harris poll conducted after *Furman* v. *Georgia* showed 59 percent to be in favor. See Neil Vidmar and Phoebe Ellsworth, "Public Opinion and the Death Penalty," *Stanford Law Review* 26 (June 1974): 1245–70.

64. Furman v. Georgia, at 362.

65. Ibid., at 363.

66. Ibid., at 343–44.

67. Ibid., at 358–59.

68. These are all listed in the comprehensive bibliography printed in Bowers, *Executions in America*, pp. 403–52.

69. A recent Field poll, taken after capital punishment had been judicially abolished in California, found that the proportion of Californians favoring it had increased to 74 percent. (*New York Times*, 26 March 1975, p. 47.)

70. *Toronto Globe and Mail*, 1 April 1976, p. 10.

71. Solicitor General of Canada, *Capital Punishment. . . .* (Ottawa, 1972), p. 3.

72. *Toronto Globe and Mail*, 11 March, 1976, p. 9. Within a month the solicitor general found it advisable to say publicly that the views of his adviser were not

necessarily his views, and the adviser himself found it advisable to moderate his charges against public opinion. (*Toronto Globe and Mail*, 8 April 1976.)

73. See especially Charles L. Black, Jr., *Capital Punishment: The Inevitability of Caprice and Mistake* (New York: Norton, 1974).

74. The average time now served in the United States for first-degree murder is ten years. See Twentieth Century Fund Task Force on Criminal Sentencing, *Fair and Certain Punishment* (New York: McGraw-Hill, 1976), p. 55 n. This is also the sentence recommended by the task force. (Ibid., p. 57.)

75. Camus, "Reflections on the Guillotine," pp. 221–22.

76. Giles Playfair, "Is the Death Penalty Necessary?" *Atlantic Monthly* 200 (September 1957): 31–35; reprinted in Grant A. McClellan, *Capital Punishment* (New York: Wilson, 1961), p. 128.

CHAPTER II

1. Richard R. Korn and Lloyd W. McCorkle, *Criminology and Penology* (New York: Holt, 1966), p. 405.

2. Thorsten Sellin, *The Death Penalty*, a report for the Model Penal Code Project of the American Law Institute (Philadelphia: American Law Institute, 1959), p. 15.

3. Marcello Maestro, *Cesare Beccaria and the Origins of Penal Reform* (Philadelphia: Temple University Press, 1973), p. 153.

4. David Brion Davis, "The Movement to Abolish Capital Punishment in America, 1787–1861," *American Historical Review* 63 (October 1957): 23.

5. David J. Rothman, *The Discovery of the Asylum: Social Order and Disorder in the New Republic* (Boston: Little, Brown, 1971), p. 46.

6. Ibid., p. 51.

7. William Bradford, *An Enquiry how far the Punishment of Death is Necessary in Pennsylvania* (Philadelphia: Dobson, 1793).

8. *The Works of Benjamin Franklin*, ed. Jared Sparks (Chicago: Townsend Mac-Coun, 1882), vol. 2, p. 481.

9. See Walter Berns, "The Constitution and the Migration of Slaves," *Yale Law Journal* 78 (December 1968): 203. Benjamin Rush made the same assumption.

10. Edward Livingston, "The Code of Reform and Prison Discipline," in *Complete Works of Edward Livingston on Criminal Jurisprudence* (Montclair, N.J.: Patterson Smith, 1968), vol. 1, p. 508.

11. See, for example, Bernard Mandeville, *An Enquiry into the Causes of the Frequent Executions at Tyburn* (London, 1725). Mandeville suggested that much of the intrepidity displayed on the gallows was due to the liquor consumed by the condemned. The solution was to deprive him of this source of his seeming strength and also of all sustenance save bread and water. "When we had seen an half-starved Wretch, that look'd like Death, come shivering from his Prison, and hardly able to speak or stand, get with Difficulty on the slow uncomfortable Carriage; where, at the first Rumbling of it, he should begin to weep, and as he went, to dissolve in Tears, and lose himself in incoherent Lamentations" (p.

45). And so on. This would be likely, he suggested, to have a salutary effect on observers. Mandeville's favored solution was to carry out executions in private.

12. Benjamin Rush, "An Enquiry into the Effects of Public Punishments Upon Criminals and Upon Society," in *Two Essays* (Philadelphia: Philadelphia Prison Society, 1954), p. 7.

13. Ibid., p. 10.

14. Ibid., p. 11.

15. Ibid., p. 13. Italics supplied.

16. Benjamin Rush, "An Enquiry into the Influence of Physical Causes upon the Moral Faculty," in *Two Essays on the Mind*, intro. by Eric T. Carlson (New York: Brunner/Mazel, 1972), p. 15.

17. Ibid., p. 21.

18. Ibid., p. 27.

19. Carlson, Introduction, in Rush, *Two Essays on the Mind*, p. ix.

20. Rush, "Physical Causes," p. 36.

21. Ibid., p. 37.

22. Gustave de Beaumont and Alexis de Tocqueville, *On the Penitentiary System in the United States and Its Application in France*, trans. Francis Lieber (Carbondale, Ill.: Southern Illinois University Press, 1964), p. 38.

23. Ibid., p. 82.

24. Lieber, Translator's Preface, in Beaumont and Tocqueville, *On the Penitentiary System*, pp. 5–6.

25. Beaumont and Tocqueville, *On the Penitentiary System*, p. 197, n. 34.

26. Ibid., p. 80.

27. Ibid., p. 89.

28. Charles Dickens, *American Notes for General Circulation*, in *Works* (New York: G. Routledge, 1850 [?]), vol. 11, pp. 284–85.

29. Ibid., p. 288.

30. Dickens's account is said to be, in part, a product of his "fertile imagination," and was immediately challenged by friends of the system. See Negley K. Teeters and John D. Shearer, *The Prison at Philadelphia: Cherry Hill* (New York: Columbia University Press, 1957), pp. 113–32. But "friends of the system" are frequently inclined to take umbrage at criticism leveled against it.

31. Beaumont and Tocqueville, *On the Penitentiary System*, p. 89.

32. Ibid.

33. Rush, "Public Punishments," p. 11.

34. See Rothman, *Discovery of the Asylum*, p. 240.

35. Ibid., p. 249.

36. Num. 35:33.

37. Gabriel de Tarde, *Penal Philosophy*, trans. Rapelje Howell (Boston: Little, Brown, 1912), p. 486.

38. See, for example, Walter Berns, *The First Amendment and the Future of American Democracy* (New York: Basic Books, 1976), ch. 1.

39. Municipal Court of Chicago, *Research Studies of Crime as Related to Heredity* (Chicago: City Hall, 1925), pp. 9, 25. For a general account of the eugenics movement in America, see Mark H. Haller, *Eugenics: Hereditarian Attitudes in American Thought* (New Brunswick, N.J.: Rutgers University Press, 1963), and especially pp. 40 ff. for an account of eugenics and criminal anthropology.

40. For a comprehensive discussion of this sterilization program, see Walter

Berns, *"Buck* v. *Bell:* Due Process of Law?" *Western Political Quarterly* 6 (December 1953): 762–75.

41. Buck v. Bell, 274 U.S. 200, 207 (1927).

42. Skinner v. Oklahoma, 316 U.S. 535 (1942).

43. Garry Wills, review of *A Time to Die* by Tom Wicker, *New York Review of Books,* 3 April 1975, p. 3.

44. According to Russell G. Oswald's *Attica—My Story* (New York: Doubleday, 1972), p. 7, 89 percent of the Attica inmates at the time of the 1971 riot had previous adult criminal records, and 58 percent had previously served time in federal and state institutions.

In 1970, 11,060 persons were admitted to federal prisons of all types. Of these, well over half for whom information was reported had known prior commitments. The breakdown is 4,779 with known prior commitments, 3,088 without known prior commitments, and 3,193 not reported. Of the 4,779 who had been in prison before, 3,909 had three or more prior commitments. (U.S. Department of Justice, Law Enforcement Assistance Administration, National Criminal Justice Information and Statistics Service, *Sourcebook of Criminal Justice Statistics,* 1973 [Washington, D.C.: U.S. Government Printing Office, 1973], p. 373.

The former director of the federal prisons, James V. Bennett, in *I Chose Prison* (New York: Knopf, 1970), p. 13, says that 70 percent of the men sent to federal prisons have previous convictions.

Daniel Glaser, in *The Effectiveness of a Prison and Parole System* (Indianapolis: Bobbs-Merrill, 1964), p. 3, says that nine-tenths of the inmates of federal and state prisons have a record of crime or juvenile delinquency before being convicted for the crime for which they are being incarcerated; half of them have been in prison before.

45. Wills, review of *A Time to Die,* p. 8.

46. Prisons differ in some very important respects, and it is a mistake to overlook these differences. The long-time director of the Federal Bureau of Prisons, James V. Bennett, succeeded in making the federal system a model for the states to emulate. He himself was a model public official. See Bennett, *I Chose Prison,* esp. pp. 37, 45, 197–229.

See also Austin MacCormick, "Adult Correctional Institutions in the United States," prepared for the President's Commission on Law Enforcement and the Administration of Justice (1967), pp. 36 ff.

47. John Bartlow Martin, *Break Down the Walls* (New York: Ballantine Books, 1954).

48. Jessica Mitford, *Kind and Usual Punishment: The Prison Business* (New York: Knopf, 1973), p. 285; cf. p. 273.

49. William J. Nagel, *The New Red Barn: A Critical Look at the Modern American Prison,* published for the American Foundation, Inc., Institute of Corrections (New York: Walker, 1973), p. 148.

50. Ramsey Clark, *Crime in America: Observations on Its Nature, Causes, Prevention, and Control* (New York: Simon & Schuster, 1970), pp. 220, 215, and 21. Italics in original.

51. *Newsweek,* 10 February 1975, p. 36.

52. Robert Martinson, "What Works?—Questions and Answers about Prison Reform," *The Public Interest,* Spring 1974, p. 49. This study is reported in much greater detail and at much greater length in Douglas S. Lipton, Robert Martin-

son, and Judith Wilks, *The Effectiveness of Correctional Treatment: A Survey of Treatment Evaluation Studies* (New York: Praeger, 1975). "What Works?" is reprinted, along with two critiques of it and a devastating response by Martinson to the critiques, in Robert Martinson, Ted Palmer, and Stuart Adams, *Rehabilitation, Recidivism, and Research* (Hackensack, N.J.: National Council on Crime and Delinquency, 1976).

53. Martinson, "What Works?" p. 44. The same conclusions were drawn independently by James Robison and Gerald Smith, "The Effectiveness of Correctional Programs," *Crime and Delinquency* 17 (January 1971): 69. Martinson's findings were also confirmed by Robert Fishman in "An Evaluation of Eighteen Projects Providing Rehabilitation and Diversion Services," in Sir Leon Radzinowicz and Marvin E. Wolfgang, eds., *Crime and Justice*, vol. 3, *The Criminal under Restraint* (New York: Basic Books, 1977), pp. 45–76.

54. Beaumont and Tocqueville, *On the Penitentiary System*, p. 89.

55. Irvin Waller, *Men Released from Prison* (Toronto: University of Toronto Press, 1974), p. 199.

56. Citizens' Inquiry on Parole and Criminal Justice, Inc. (Ramsey Clark, chairman), "Summary Report on New York Parole" (March 1974), p. 5 and passim.

57. Benjamin Karpman, "Criminality, Insanity, and the Law," *Journal of Criminal Law, Criminology and Police Science* 39 (January-February 1949): 584.

58. Ibid., p. 605.

59. Thomas S. Szasz, M.D., "The Sane Slave: Social Control and Legal Psychiatry," *American Criminal Law Review* 10 (1972): 353.

60. Ibid., p. 355.

61. Bruce J. Ennis and Thomas R. Litwack, "Psychiatry and the Presumption of Expertise: Flipping Coins in the Courtroom," *California Law Review* 62 (1974): 701–2, 713, 748.

62. Alan M. Dershowitz, "The Psychiatrist's Power in Civil Commitment: A Knife that Cuts Both Ways," *Psychology Today* 2 (1969): 47.

63. Ennis and Litwack, "Psychiatry and the Presumption of Expertise," p. 695.

64. See Richard V. Ericson, "Psychiatrists in Prisons: On Admitting Professional Tinkers in a Tinkers' Paradise," *Chitty's Law Journal* 22 (1974): 29–33. The program is reported in Solicitor General of Canada, *The General Program for the Development of Psychiatric Services in Federal Correctional Services in Canada* (Ottawa, 1973).

65. Karpman, "Criminality, Insanity, and the Law," p. 590.

66. Gary S. Becker, "Crime and Punishment: An Economic Approach," in Becker and William M. Landes, eds., *Essays in the Economics of Crime and Punishment* (New York: National Bureau of Economic Research, 1974), p. 9.

67. Sigmund Freud, *Civilization and Its Discontents*, trans. Joan Riviere (London: Hogarth Press, 1957), pp. 105–13.

68. Edwin H. Sutherland and Donald R. Cressey, *Principles of Criminology*, 7th ed. (Philadelphia and New York: Lippincott, 1966), p. 370.

69. Martinson, "What Works?" p. 49.

70. American Friends Service Committee, *Struggle for Justice* (New York: Hill & Wang, 1971), p. v.

71. Norval Morris, "The Future of Imprisonment: Toward a Punitive Philosophy," *Michigan Law Review* 72 (May 1974): 1161, 1174.

72. Andrew von Hirsch, *Doing Justice: The Choice of Punishments,* report of the Committee for the Study of Incarceration (New York: Hill & Wang, 1976), p. xxxix.

73. Sellin, *Death Penalty,* p. 15.

74. American Friends Service Committee, *Struggle for Justice,* p. 10.

75. Tom Wicker, *A Time to Die* (New York: Quadrangle, 1975), p. 203.

76. Karl Menninger, M.D., *The Crime of Punishment* (New York: Viking, 1969), p. 9.

77. Ibid., p. 153. Italics in original.

78. Ibid., p. 190.

79. *American Journal of Corrections* 37 (July-August 1975): 32. The award was announced by the twenty-second National Institute on Crime and Delinquency.

80. Menninger, *Crime of Punishment,* pp. 4 and 5.

81. Ibid., p. 113.

82. Ibid.

83. Friedrich Nietzsche, *Beyond Good and Evil,* trans. Walter Kaufmann (New York: Vintage, 1966), sec. 201. Italics in original.

84. American Friends Service Committee, *Struggle for Justice,* p. 18.

85. Ibid., p. 43.

86. Ibid., pp. 44–45.

87. Wicker, *A Time to Die,* pp. 248–49.

88. Francis A. Allen, "The Rehabilitative Ideal," in Rudolph J. Gerber and Patrick D. McAnany, eds., *Contemporary Justice: Views, Explanations, and Justifications* (Notre Dame, Ind.: University of Notre Dame Press, 1972), p. 211.

89. *Toronto Globe and Mail,* 16 June 1976, p. 7.

CHAPTER III

1. Max Weber, *On Law in Economy and Society,* ed. Max Rheinstein (Cambridge, Mass.: Harvard University Press, 1954), pp. 50 ff.

2. Thomas Hobbes, *Leviathan,* pt. 1, chap. 14.

3. Ibid., pt. 2, chap. 29. Italics in original.

4. Ibid., pt. 1, chap. 15.

5. Cesare Beccaria, *On Crimes and Punishments,* trans. Henry Paolucci (Indianapolis: Bobbs-Merrill, Library of Liberal Arts, 1963), p. 94.

6. Ibid., p. 65. Italics in original. See also pp. 96–97.

7. Hobbes, *Leviathan,* pt. 2, chap. 30.

8. Beccaria, *On Crimes and Punishments,* p. 42.

9. Ibid., p. 30.

10. Ibid., p. 63.

11. Edmund Burke, *Reflections on the Revolution in France,* in *Works* (London: C. and J. Rivington, 1826), vol. 5, p. 152.

12. Anthony Amsterdam in oral argument in Gregg v. Georgia, Supreme Court of the United States, #74-6257. *New York Times,* 1 April 1976, p. 1.

13. Thorsten Sellin, *The Death Penalty,* a report for the Model Penal Code Project of the American Law Institute (Philadelphia: American Law Institute, 1959), p. 63.

14. Norval Morris and Gordon Hawkins, "From Murder and Violence, Good Lord, Deliver Us," *Midway* 10 (Summer 1969): 85.

15. Gordon Tullock, "Does Punishment Deter Crime?" *The Public Interest,* Summer 1974, p. 107.

16. Hugo Adam Bedau, "Deterrence and the Death Penalty: A Reconsideration," *Journal of Criminal Law, Criminology and Police Science* 61 (1970): 546.

17. Walter Reckless, *The Crime Problem,* 4th ed. (New York: Appleton-Century-Crofts, 1962), p. 508.

18. William J. Bowers, *Executions in America* (Lexington, Mass.: Heath, 1974), p. 195.

19. Paul W. Tappan, *Crime, Justice and Correction* (New York: McGraw-Hill, 1960), p. 245. Also see Maynard L. Erickson and Jack P. Gibbs, "The Deterrence Question: Some Alternative Methods of Analysis," *Social Science Quarterly* 54, no. 3 (December 1973): 534–51.

20. Great Britain, Royal Commission on Capital Punishment (1949–53), *Report* (London: H. M. Stationery Office, Cmd. 8932), p. 22.

21. Robert Martinson, Letter to the Editor, *Commentary* 58 (October 1974): 12.

22. Ezzat A. Fattah, "The Canadian Experiment with Abolition of the Death Penalty," in Bowers, *Executions in America,* p. 133. This paper is a summary of his report to the solicitor general. See Fattah, *A Study of the Deterrent Effect of Capital Punishment with Special Reference to the Canadian Situation* (Ottawa: Department of the Solicitor General, 1972).

23. Fattah, "Canadian Experiment," p. 134.

24. Ibid., p. 121.

25. Karl F. Schuessler, "The Deterrent Influence of the Death Penalty," *Annals of the American Academy of Political and Social Science* 284 (1952): 61.

26. Ibid., p. 60.

27. This negative association "turns out to be significant statistically at the five percent level for a one-tail test." (Isaac Ehrlich, "Deterrence: Evidence and Inference," *Yale Law Journal* 85 [December 1975], p. 221, n. 35.) What this means is that in random sampling from a population with a zero coefficient of simple correlation a value of −0.26 or smaller would occur only five (or fewer) times out of a hundred due to *pure* chance.

28. Schuessler, "Deterrent Influence," p. 60.

29. Bowers, *Executions in America,* p. 145.

30. Ehrlich, "Deterrence: Evidence and Inference," p. 223.

31. Bowers, *Executions in America,* p. 163.

32. Editorial, *Toronto Globe and Mail,* 26 February 1976.

33. Hugo Adam Bedau, "Deterrence and the Death Penalty," pp. 546, 547.

34. Ibid., p. 548.

35. Fowler v. North Carolina, Supreme Court of the United States, #73–7031. Brief for the United States as Amicus Curiae, p. 36.

36. Isaac Ehrlich, "The Deterrent Effect of Capital Punishment: A Question of Life and Death," *American Economic Review* 65 (June 1975): 398.

37. *Washington Post,* 13 April 1975, pp. A–1 ff.

38. *Los Angeles Times,* 5 May 1975, p. 1.

39. *Washington Post,* 13 April 1975, p. A–1.

40. Isaac Ehrlich, "Participation in Illegitimate Activities: A Theoretical and Empirical Investigation," *Journal of Political Economy* 81 (May-June 1973): 521–65.

41. Ehrlich, "Deterrent Effect of Capital Punishment," p. 407.

42. Ibid., pp. 413–14.

43. Ibid., p. 414.

44. Fowler v. North Carolina, Supreme Court of the United States, #73–7031. Reply Brief for the Petitioner, Appendix C, p. 4.

45. Peter Passell and John B. Taylor, "The Deterrent Effect of Capital Punishment: Another View," Columbia University Discussion Paper 74–7509 (March 1975). This paper is printed as Appendix E to the Reply Brief for the Petitioner. See above, note 44.

46. Peter Passell, "The Deterrent Effect of the Death Penalty: A Statistical Test," *Stanford Law Review* 28 (November 1975): 79, 80.

47. Ibid., p. 79.

48. Ehrlich, "Deterrence: Evidence and Inference," pp. 219, 227.

49. David C. Baldus and James W. L. Cole, "A Comparison of the Work of Thorsten Sellin and Isaac Ehrlich on the Deterrent Effect of Capital Punishment," *Yale Law Journal* 85 (December 1975): 174, 186.

50. Hans Zeisel, "The Deterrent Effect of the Death Penalty: Facts and Faith," *The Supreme Court Review, 1976,* ed. Philip B. Kurland (Chicago: University of Chicago Press, 1977), p. 336.

51. Isaac Ehrlich, "Capital Punishment and Deterrence: Some Further Thoughts and Additional Evidence," *Journal of Political Economy* 85, no. 4 (August 1977): 742.

52. Peter Passell and John B. Taylor, "The Deterrent Effect of Capital Punishment: Another View," *American Economic Review* 67, no. 3 (June 1977): 450. This is a revised version of their workshop paper (see above, note 45). Ehrlich, conceding nothing to Passell and Taylor, responded to their criticism in the same issue of the *Review.*

That we cannot yet know whether capital punishment deters murder is also the conclusion of a still more recent evaluation conducted under the auspices of the National Academy of Sciences: "In summary, the flaws in the earlier analyses (i.e., Sellin's and others) and the sensitivity of the more recent analysis to minor variations in model specification and the serious temporal instability of the results lead the panel to conclude that the available studies provide no useful evidence on the deterrent effect of capital punishment." Alfred Blumstein, Jacqueline Cohen, and Daniel Nagin (eds.), *Deterrence and Incapacitation: Estimating the Effects of Criminal Sanctions on Crime Rates* (National Academy of Sciences: Washington, D.C., 1978), p. 9. See also pp. 336–60.

53. *Toronto Globe and Mail,* 1 October 1976, p. 8.

54. State of North Carolina v. Jarrette, 284 N.C. 670 (1974). See Fowler v. North Carolina, Supreme Court of the United States, #73–7031, Brief for Respondent, p. 47.

55. U.S. Department of Justice, Law Enforcement Assistance Administration, National Criminal Justice Information and Statistics Service, *Sourcebook of Criminal Justice Statistics,* 1974 (Washington, D.C.: U.S. Government Printing Office, 1975) pp. 246, 247.

56. Federal Bureau of Investigation, *Uniform Crime Reports for the United States,* 1972 (Washington, D.C.: U.S. Government Printing Office, 1972), p. 9; and *Uniform Crime Reports,* 1974, p. 19. Another 5.6 percent of the murders are of the

"suspected felony type." In 1975 the number of murders decreased slightly (to 20,510), but the proportion of felony murders increased to 23 percent, and the proportion of suspected felony murders to 9.4 percent. (*Uniform Crime Reports,* 1975, pp. 19, 49.)

57. *New York Times,* 13 June 1976, pp. 1, 60.

58. The preliminary 1977 figures show an increase in the murder rate of 1 percent over 1976. (*Uniform Crime Reports,* 1977, Preliminary Annual Release, 21 March 1978.)

59. Federal Bureau of Investigation, *Uniform Crime Reports,* 1974, p. 55; 1976, p. 37.

60. Federal Bureau of Investigation, *Uniform Crime Reports,* 1974, p. 176. These statistics are drawn from the reports of 1,496 cities. I am assuming that the same rates apply in the country as a whole.

61. U.S. Department of Justice, Law Enforcement Assistance Administration, *Criminal Victimization in the United States,* 1973 Advance Report, p. 12.

62. *Detroit Free Press,* 15 April 1974, p. 10–A.

63. U.S. Department of Justice, *Sourcebook of Criminal Justice Statistics,* 1976, p. 358.

64. U.S. Department of Justice, *Sourcebook of Criminal Justice Statistics,* 1974, p. 204.

65. Ibid., p. 396.

66. Ronald L. Goldfarb and Linda R. Singer, *After Conviction* (New York: Simon & Schuster, 1973), p. 209.

67. California, Board of Corrections, "Probation, Supervision, and Training," 1964, p. 5.

68. U.S. Department of Justice, *Sourcebook of Criminal Justice Statistics,* 1974, p. 396.

69. Ibid., p. 405.

70. James Q. Wilson, *Thinking about Crime* (New York: Basic Books, 1975), p. 165. The studies cited by Wilson are Martin A. Levin, "Urban Politics and Policy Outcomes: The Criminal Courts," in *Criminal Justice,* ed. George F. Cole (North Scituate, Mass.: Duxbury Press, 1972), p. 335; Dean V. Babst and John W. Mannering, "Probation versus Imprisonment for Similar Types of Offenders," *Journal of Research in Crime and Delinquency* 2 (July 1965): 61 ff.; and Peter W. Greenwood et al., *Prosecution of Adult Felony Defendants in Los Angeles County: A Policy Perspective,* Report No. R–1127–DOJ (Santa Monica, Calif.: Rand Corporation, 1973), p. 109.

71. Wilson, *Thinking about Crime,* pp. 434, 471. There were 212,953 prisoners in 1960 and 204,349 in 1973.

72. The number of prisoners at the end of 1974 was 218,466; by the end of 1975 the number had increased to 242,750, an increase of 24,284, the largest ever recorded in a year. U.S. Department of Justice, Law Enforcement Assistance Administration, NPS Bulletin, *Prisoners in State and Federal Institutions on December 31, 1975,* pp. 1, 16.

73. American Law Institute, *Model Penal Code,* proposed final draft (Philadelphia, 30 July 1962), p. 106. The relevant section reads as follows:

Section 7.01 Criteria for Withholding Sentence of Imprisonment and for Placing Defendant on Probation.

(1) The Court shall deal with a person who has been convicted of a crime

without imposing sentence of imprisonment unless, having regard to the nature and circumstances of the crime and the history, character and condition of the defendant, it is of the opinion that his imprisonment is necessary for protection of the public because

(a) there is undue risk that during the period of a suspended sentence or probation the defendant will commit another crime; or

(b) the defendant is in need of correctional treatment that can be provided most effectively by his commitment to an institution; or

(c) a lesser sentence will depreciate the seriousness of the defendant's crime.

74. National Council on Crime and Delinquency, Council of Judges, Model Sentencing Act, art. 1. This is published in full, with accompanying comments, in *Crime and Delinquency* 18 (1972): 335–70. The quoted statements are both found on p. 344.

75. Marvin E. Frankel, *Criminal Sentences: Law without Order* (New York: Hill & Wang, 1973), p. 5.

76. Ibid., p. 58.

77. Ibid., p. 89 and passim.

78. Twentieth Century Fund Task Force on Criminal Sentencing, *Fair and Certain Punishment* (New York: McGraw-Hill, 1976), pp. vii, 33.

79. Lewis Katz (with Lawrence Litwin and Richard Bamberger), *Justice Is the Crime: Pretrial Delay in Felony Cases* (Cleveland and London: Press of Case Western Reserve University, 1972), p. 2.

80. Great Britain, Lord Chancellor's Department, *Statistics on Judicial Administration* (London: H.M. Stationery Office, 1973), pp. 6, 38.

81. Katz, *Justice Is the Crime,* pp. 36–37.

82. People v. Esparza, Cal. 2d Crim. No. 18326 (1971).

83. Macklin Fleming, *The Price of Perfect Justice: The Adverse Consequences of Current Legal Doctrine on the American Courtroom* (New York: Basic Books, 1974), pp. 67–69.

84. Katz, *Justice Is the Crime,* pp. 42, 76–77.

85. They are paid more for a case that is tried, but the differential is not enough to justify the necessity to accept fewer cases. Trials are time-consuming. See Katz, *Justice Is the Crime,* pp. 71–72.

86. Ibid., p. 69.

87. Ibid., p. 79.

88. Fleming, *Price of Perfect Justice,* p. 27.

89. Dombrowski v. Pfister, 380 U.S. 479 (1965). This was limited in Younger v. Harris, 401 U.S. 37 (1971).

90. In the 1973–74 term, 2,118 *in forma pauperis* cases (most of them involving prisoners) were docketed, and the Court had not dealt with 467 from the previous term. 94 S.Ct. *218.* There will probably be fewer of these cases (i.e., appeals from denials of habeas corpus) as the result of the Court's decision in *Stone* v. *Powell,* 96 S.Ct. 3037 (1976).

91. Fleming, *Price of Perfect Justice,* pp. 28–29.

92. Bates and Chavez v. Nelson, 485 F 2d 90 (1973); Chavez v. McCarthy, 94 S.Ct. 877 (1974).

93. Gideon v. Wainwright, 372 U.S. 335 (1963).

94. Fleming, *Price of Perfect Justice,* p. 15.

95. Ibid., p. 29.
96. *Toronto Globe and Mail,* 12 February 1976, p. 1.
97. Mapp v. Ohio, 367 U.S. 643 (1961).
98. Miranda v. Arizona, 384 U.S. 436 (1966).
99. Leonard W. Levy, *Against the Law: The Nixon Court and Criminal Justice* (New York: Harper & Row, 1974), pp. 70–71.
100. Fleming, *Price of Perfect Justice,* pp. 31–36.
101. Sanders v. United States, 373 U.S. 1, 8 (1963).
102. *Annual Report of the Director of the Administrative Office of the United States Courts,* 1974 (Washington, D.C.: U.S. Government Printing Office, 1975), pp. 189–289.
103. *Criminal Statistics, England and Wales,* 1974 (London: H.M. Stationery Office, 1975, Cmnd. 6168), pp. 227, 234.
104. Leonard Levy admits that the criminal justice system is "grinding to a halt and is in danger of massive breakdown," but he refuses to blame the Warren Court—even though its decisions "tended to make convictions more difficult to get, verdicts of guilty [more] difficult to [make] stick, and sentences more difficult to execute." He attributes the imminent breakdown to the "staggering rise in the number of crimes and the resultant congestion of prosecutorial case loads and court dockets." (Levy, *Against the Law,* p. 4.)
105. Downum v. United States, 372 U.S. 734 (1963).
106. Harrison v. United States, 392 U.S. 219 (1968).
107. Brown v. Allen, 344 U.S. 443, 540 (1953).
108. U.S. Department of Justice, *Sourcebook of Criminal Justice Statistics,* 1974, p. 380.
109. Chief Justice Warren E. Burger, "State of the Federal Judiciary," 10 August 1970, 91 S.Ct. 7 (advance sheets).
110. Illinois v. Somerville, 410 U.S. 458 (1973).
111. "As a practical matter, the core of *Miranda* . . . remains largely intact. From the standpoint of candor and craftsmanship, however, the opinions, taken as a whole, are highly unsatisfactory. In its unyielding determination to reach the desired result, the Court has too often resorted to distortion of the record, disregard of the precedents, and an unwillingness honestly to explain or to justify its conclusions." (Geoffrey R. Stone, "The Miranda Doctrine in the Burger Court," *The Supreme Court Review,* 1977, ed. Philip B. Kurland [Chicago: University of Chicago Press, 1978], p. 169.) Stone predicts that the Burger Court will "gradually dismantle *Miranda* piecemeal."
112. Harris v. New York, 401 U.S. 222 (1971). See also Michigan v. Tucker, 417 U.S. 433 (1974); Michigan v. Moseley, 96 S.Ct. 321 (1975); Beckwith v. United States, 96 S.Ct. 1612 (1976); United States v. Mandujano, 96 S.Ct. 1768 (1976).
113. United States v. MacCollom, 96 S.Ct. 2086 (1976). See also Francis v. Henderson, 96 S.Ct. 1708 (1976).

CHAPTER IV

1. Jack P. Gibbs, *Crime, Punishment, and Deterrence* (New York: Elsevier, 1975), p. ix.
2. Fyodor Dostoevsky, *The House of the Dead*, trans. Constance Garnett (New York: Grove Press, 1957), p. 52.
3. Ibid., p. 97. Italics in original.
4. Cesare Beccaria, *On Crimes and Punishments*, trans. Henry Paolucci (Indianapolis: Bobbs-Merrill, Library of Liberal Arts, 1963), p. 95.
5. Ibid., p. 94.
6. Ibid., p. 44.
7. Thomas Babington Macaulay, *Critical and Historical Essays* (London: Everyman's, 1951), vol. 2, p. 373.
8. Beccaria, *On Crimes and Punishments*, p. 77, n. 40.
9. Ibid., p. 95.
10. Fyodor Dostoevsky, *Notes from Underground*, in *Notes from Underground, Poor People, and The Friend of the Family*, trans. Constance Garnett (New York: Dell, 1969), p. 41.
11. Thomas Hobbes, *Leviathan*, part 1, chap. 15. Italics in original.
12. Jean-Jacques Rousseau, *Emile*, in *Oeuvres Complètes* (Dijon: Pléiades, 1969), vol. 4, p. 523 n.
13. Beccaria, *On Crimes and Punishments*, p. 46.
14. Ibid., pp. 47, 49.
15. Ibid., p. 47.
16. Ibid., p. 42.
17. Hobbes, *Leviathan*, part 2, chap. 21.
18. John Locke, *Second Treatise of Civil Government*, chap. 2, sec. 6. Italics supplied.
19. Jean-Jacques Rousseau, *Narcisse, ou L'Amant de Lui-Même* (Préface), in *Oeuvres Complètes* (Dijon: Pléiades, 1961), vol. 2, p. 971.
20. Hobbes, *Leviathan*, pt. 2, chap. 29.
21. Walter Berns, *The First Amendment and the Future of American Democracy* (New York: Basic Books, 1976), chap. 1.
22. Hobbes, *Leviathan*, part 2, chap. 30. Locke's views were similar: "For the private judgment of any person concerning a law enacted in political matters, for the public good, does not take away the obligation of that law, nor deserve a dispensation." *A Letter Concerning Toleration*, in *Works* (1812 ed.), vol. 6, p. 43.
23. Beccaria, *On Crimes and Punishments*, p. 41.
24. Ibid., p. 94.
25. John Stuart Mill, *On Liberty*, chap. 1, "Introductory."
26. This is the conclusion drawn by law professor Walter Barnett. See his *Sexual Freedom and the Constitution: An Inquiry into the Constitutionality of Repressive Sex Laws* (Albuquerque, N.Mex.: University of New Mexico Press, 1973), pp. 12–13.
27. Alexis de Tocqueville, *Democracy in America* (New York: Vintage, 1945), vol. 2, pp. 154–55.
28. On the intent of the religious provisions of the First Amendment, see Berns, *First Amendment*, chap. 1; on the issue of religious education in the public

schools, see chap. 2; on obscenity and related issues, chap. 5, which also includes a discussion of the family's role. The obscenity case referred to is United States v. Limehouse, 285 U.S. 424 (1932).

29. Engel v. Vitale, 370 U.S. 421 (1962); Abington School District v. Schempp, 374 U.S. 203 (1963); Meek v. Pittinger, 95 S.Ct. 1753 (1975); A Book . . . v. Attorney General, 383 U.S. 413 (1966); Cohen v. California, 403 U.S. 15 (1971); Rosenfeld v. New Jersey, 408 U.S. 901 (1972); Papish v. Board of Curators, 410 U.S. 667 (1973); West Virginia State Board of Education v. Barnette, 319 U.S. 624 (1943); Street v. New York, 394 U.S. 576 (1969); Smith v. Goguen, 94 S.Ct. 1242 (1974); Spence v. Washington, 94 S.Ct. 2727 (1974).

30. Johannes Andenaes, "General Prevention—Illusion or Reality?" *Journal of Criminal Law, Criminology and Police Science* 43 (July-August 1952): 179.

31. Ibid., p. 197.

32. C. S. Lewis, *God in the Dock: Essays on Theology and Ethics,* ed. Walter Hooper (Grand Rapids, Mich.: William B. Eerdmans, 1970), p. 288.

33. A. L. Goodhart, *English Law and the Moral Law* (London: Stevens & Sons, 1953), pp. 92–93.

34. Ps. 32:10–11.

35. *New York Times,* 26 August 1973, sec. 4, p. 6.

36. Johannes Andenaes, *Punishment and Deterrence,* with a foreword by Norval Morris (Ann Arbor, Mich.: University of Michigan Press, 1974), p. 133.

37. Adam Smith, *The Theory of Moral Sentiments* (New York: A. M. Kelley, 1966), p. 95.

38. Andenaes, *Punishment and Deterrence,* p. 133.

39. Hobbes, *Leviathan,* pt. 1, chap. 10.

40. Locke, *Second Treatise,* secs. 37, 40, 41, 43.

41. Sir James Fitzjames Stephen, *A History of the Criminal Law of England* (London, 1883; New York: Burt Franklin, n.d.), vol. 2, p. 82.

CHAPTER V

1. Aristotle *Rhetoric* 1378b1–5.

2. Ibid., 1381a4–6.

3. Albert Camus, *Carnets-II,* January 1942–March 1951 (Paris: Gallimard, 1964), p. 31.

4. Ibid.

5. Ibid., p. 30.

6. Jean-Paul Sartre, "Réponse à Albert Camus," *Les Temps Modernes* 8 (August 1952): 345.

7. Albert Camus, "Reflections on the Guillotine," in *Resistance, Rebellion, and Death,* trans. Justin O'Brien (New York: Knopf, 1961), pp. 220, 222.

8. Albert Camus, *The Rebel,* trans. Anthony Bower (New York: Knopf, 1971).

9. Camus, "Reflections on the Guillotine," p. 222.

10. Abe Fortas, "The Case against Capital Punishment," *New York Times Magazine,* 23 January 1977, p. 29.

11. Furman v. Georgia, 408 U.S. 238, 273 (1972). He quoted this statement four years later in his dissent in *Gregg* v. *Georgia,* 96 S.Ct. 2909, 2972 (1976).

12. Lincoln to James H. Hackett, 17 August 1863, *The Collected Works of Abraham Lincoln,* ed. Roy P. Basler (New Brunswick, N.J.: Rutgers University Press, 1953), vol. 6, p. 393.

13. William Shakespeare, *Macbeth,* act 1, sc. 7, lines 12–16.

14. Winston S. Churchill, *The Second World War: The Gathering Storm* (Boston: Houghton Mifflin, 1948), p. 667.

15. Shakespeare, *Macbeth,* act 4, sc. 3, lines 216–19.

16. Ibid., act 2, sc. 2, lines 60–63.

17. Aristotle *Poetics* 1448a–1.

18. Thomas L. Pangle, "The Political Psychology of Religion in Plato's *Laws,*" *American Political Science Review* 70 (December 1976): 1062.

19. U.S. Congress, *The Debates and Proceedings in the Congress of the United States, 1789–1824,* 42 vols., known as *The Annals of Congress* (Gales & Seaton, 1834–56), vol. 1, pp. 451, 790.

20. West Virginia State Board of Education v. Barnette, 319 U.S. 624, 670 (1943). Dissenting opinion.

21. Ableman v. Booth, 21 Howard 506 (1859).

22. Jaffa, *Crisis of the House Divided,* chap. 9, esp. pp. 225–32.

23. G. W. F. Hegel, *Philosophy of Right,* trans. T. M. Knox (London: Oxford University Press, 1967), sec. 324 (pp. 209–10).

24. Trop v. Dulles, 356 U.S. 86, 122 (1958). Dissenting opinion.

25. Affroyim v. Rusk, 387 U.S. 253 (1967). Expatriation and banishment are not equivalent terms. "Expatriation" means loss of citizenship but not necessarily expulsion from the country.

26. Cesare Beccaria, *On Crimes and Punishments,* trans. Henry Paolucci (Indianapolis: Bobbs-Merrill, Library of Liberal Arts, 1963), p. 53.

27. U.S. Department of Justice, Law Enforcement Assistance Administration, National Criminal Justice Information and Statistics Service, *Expenditure and Employment Data for the Criminal Justice System,* 1974 (Washington, D.C.: U.S. Government Printing Office, 1976), p. 2. The 1974 total was $16,279,000,000, broken down as follows: federal, $2,603,000,000; state, $4,546,000,000; and local, $9,130,000,000.

28. Jean-Jacques Rousseau, *Emile,* in *Oeuvres Complètes* (Dijon: Pléiades, 1969), vol. 4, p. 633 (footnote at the end of the Savoyard Vicar section).

CHAPTER VI

1. Arthur Koestler, *Reflections on Hanging* (London: Gollancz, 1956), p. 164.

2. Gregg v. Georgia, 96 S.Ct. 2909; Jurek v. Texas, 96 S.Ct. 2950; Proffitt v. Florida, 96 S.Ct. 2960 (1976). There was no opinion for the court in these cases; the explicit support for the retributive principle appears in the opinion of Justice Potter Stewart, announcing the judgment of the Court, and joined by Justices Lewis F. Powell, Jr. and John Paul Stevens.

3. Gregg v. Georgia, at 2976–77. Dissenting opinion.

4. Hugo Adam Bedau, "The Death Penalty in America," *Federal Probation* 35 (June 1971): 36. There apparently have been cases in America where innocent persons have been convicted of capital crimes, but, as Bedau acknowledges, they were sentenced to prison, not executed.

5. Franklin E. Zimring, Joel Eigen, and Sheila O'Malley, "Punishing Homicide in Philadelphia: Perspectives on the Death Penalty," *University of Chicago Law Review* 43, no. 2 (Winter 1976): 251, 252.

6. Note, "Discretion and the Constitutionality of the New Death Penalty Statutes," *Harvard Law Review* 87 (1974): 1691–92.

7. Charles L. Black, Jr., *Capital Punishment: The Inevitability of Caprice and Mistake* (New York: Norton, 1974).

8. Ibid., p. 66.

9. *Newsweek*, 21 March 1977, p. 21.

10. Woodson v. North Carolina, 96 S.Ct. 2978; Roberts v. Louisiana, 96 S.Ct. 3001 (1976).

11. Proffitt v. Florida, at 2967.

12. The Supreme Court has not forbidden the death penalty for all rapes. Its judgment in Coker v. Georgia, 97 S.Ct. 2861 (1977), was that the death sentence is an excessive punishment for the crime of rape of an adult woman.

13. Lockett v. Ohio, 57 L Ed 2d 973; Bell v. Ohio, 57 L Ed 2d 1010 (1978).

14. " . . . we conclude that the Eighth and Fourteenth Amendments require that the sentencer, in all but the rarest kind of capital case, not be precluded from considering *as a mitigating factor,* any aspect of a defendant's character or record and any of the circumstances of the offense that the defendant proffers as a basis for a sentence less than death." Lockett v. Ohio, at p. 990.

15. Lockett v. Ohio, at p. 1006.

16. Furman v. Georgia, 408 U.S. 238, 249 (1972). He was quoting the President's Commission on Law Enforcement and the Administration of Justice, *The Challenge of Crime in a Free Society* (1967), p. 143.

17. Furman v. Georgia, 408 U.S. 238 (1972), at 389–90, n. 12.

18. U.S. Department of Justice, Law Enforcement Assistance Administration, National Criminal Justice Information and Statistics Service, *Capital Punishment, 1974*, National Prisoner Statistics Bulletin No. SD-NPS-CP-3 (Washington, D.C.: U.S. Government Printing Office, 1975), pp. 20–21.

19. Ibid., p. 45.

20. Marc Riedel, "Discrimination in the Imposition of the Death Penalty: A Comparison of the Characteristics of Offenders Sentenced Pre-*Furman* and Post-*Furman,"* *Temple Law Quarterly* 49, no. 2 (Winter 1976): 276. Riedel says (p. 278) that the proportion of nonwhites sentenced to death continues to be higher in the South than in any other region, but he is contradicted by his own statistics. The proportion in the South is now 63 percent (p. 277), whereas in the Northeast (Rhode Island, New York, and Pennsylvania) it is 100 percent (p. 276). It should be added that only three persons make up this 100 percent, but these three were indeed nonwhite.

21. Ibid., p. 283.

22. Marvin Wolfgang and Marc Riedel, "Race, Judicial Discretion, and the Death Penalty," *Annals of the American Academy of Political and Social Science* 407 (May 1973): 119–33.

23. He cites two other sources: Black, *Capital Punishment*, and Note, "New

Death Penalty Statutes," p. 1694, n. 23. But neither of these provides any evidence of racial discrimination in the post-*Furman* period. On the contrary, the latter speaks of the difficulty of proving racially discriminatory sentencing, especially in the light of the higher black crime rate.

24. Federal Bureau of Investigation, *Uniform Crime Reports*, 1974 (Washington, D.C.: U.S. Government Printing Office, 1974), p. 19.

25. Edmund Wilson, *Patriotic Gore: Studies in the Literature of the American Civil War* (New York: Oxford University Press, 1962), p. 130.

INDEX

Abolition, 11–35; biblical argument for, 11–18; constitutional argument for, 31–35 (*see also* Constitution; Supreme Court; *and specific amendments*); deterrence argument and, 28–31 (*see also* Deterrence); dignity of man argument for, 24–28, 75, 162–63, 189; immorality of, 156–63; natural public law argument for, 18–24, 38, 84; progress toward, 3–5; *See also* Liberal society; Reform

Administration: of death penalty, 177–89; *See also* Courts; Juries; Law, the; Supreme Court

Alembert, Jean Le Rond d', 42

Allen, Francis, 80

Allmand, Warren, 37, 71

Andenaes, Johannes, 143–45, 147, 149, 152

André, Major John, 31, 162

Anger, 12, 146–50, 175, 187; Beccaria's view of, 149, 150; combined with compassion for victims, 81; as desire for revenge, 137–38; as hypocritical, 156–58; in moral community, 153–56; role of, in inflicting punishment, 147

Appeal, right of, 117–19, 121–22, 124–26

Argyle, earl of, 17

Aristotle, 166

Arnold, Benedict, 31

Attica, 57, 61, 63, 76, 79–80

Auburn system, 51, 52, 54, 57

Babst, V., 110

Baldus, David, 101

Banishment (expatriation), 11, 32, 43, 45–46, 173–74

Barbarism, capital punishment associated with, 26–27

Bates (defendant), 117–19

Baxter, Richard, 15–16

Beaumont, Gustave de, 50, 52, 53, 54, 56, 57, 68

Beccaria, Cesare, 25, 75, 86; banishment opposed by, 174; decriminalization program of, 19, 43, 140–41; deterrence and, 28–29, 110; deterrence and morality of the law and, 136–38, 148–50, 152; dignity of man argument and, 24; and enlightened self-interest, 131–33; influence of, 41–45, 84; life imprisonment and, 39, 135; and morality outside the law, 189; natural public law argument and, 18–23, 38; on need for infallible punishment, 113; on need for simple and clear laws, 130; and purpose of punishment, 85, 87; on reasons for inflicting death penalty, 134–35

Bedau, Hugo Adam, 91, 97, 98, 178

Behavior modification programs, 69

Benefit of clergy, 33

Bentham, Jeremy, 22

Biblical argument: in support of abolition, 11–18

Bill of Rights (1791), 170; *See also specific amendments*

Bixby, Mrs., 162

Black, Charles, 179–81

Blackmun, Harry A., 4

Blacks: imposition of death penalty on, 33–35, 185–87

Bork, Robert H., 97

Bormann, Martin, 8

Bourgeois society, *see* Liberal society

Bowers, William J., 91, 96

Bradford, William, 44

Branch, Elmer, 34

Brandeis, Louis, 126

Brennan, William J., Jr., 27, 35, 121–22, 162, 163, 189

Britain, *see* England

Brown, Jerry, 65

Burger, Warren, 4, 118, 125

Burger Court, 126, 127

Burke, Edmund, 86

Index

California Youth Authority Community Treatment Project, 66–68
Camus, Albert, 5, 7, 25–26, 80, 156–61, 163, 167–68
Canada, 37–38; abolition in, 4–5, 81, 92–95, 102; impanelment of juries in, 119–20; life imprisonment in, 39; rehabilitation in, 66–67, 71
Castration, 69
Charles I (King of England), 15
Charles II (King of England), 15
Chavez (defendant), 117–19
Cherry Hill penitentiary, 51–52, 63, 64, 68
Christianity, 13–19; capital punishment in name of, 15–18, 23, liberalism and, 17–18 (see also Liberal society); penitence and, 59–60
Church-state separation, 42–43, 61, 140; See also Liberal society
Churchill, Sir Winston, 166
Citizenship: loss of, as cruel and unusual punishment, 32, 173–74, 176, 186, 189
Clark, Ramsey, 52, 65, 66, 68
Cole, James, 101
Colonial America, 43–45
Commercial society, see Liberal society
Committed crime: reported vs., 108
Concealment: of executions, 25–26; See also Public executions
Conscience: Rush's definition of, 49
Constitution (U.S.), 27, 44, 124–25, 169–71, 178; See also specific amendments
Constitutional argument: in support of abolition, 31–35; See also Supreme Court
Conviction rate, 108; drop in, 125
Corll, Dean Allen, 9
Courts, 108–24; leniency of, 108–12; problems with, 112–24; See also Conviction rate; Judges; Juries; Sentences; Supreme Court; Trials
Cressey, Donald R., 72
Crime: blamed on society, 74–82; as contrary to self-interest, 138 (see also Self-interest); economic factors of, 72; moderating of law and increase in, 5–6; moral strength needed to respond to, 6–7; of passion, murder as, 104–5 (see also Murder); property, 182–83; public opinion on, 146–47; reported vs. committed, 108; See also Punishment

Crime rate: effects of capital punishment on, 30; increasing number of murders and increasing, 105–6
Criminal law, see Law, the
Criminal justice system, see Appeal, right of; Conviction rate; Courts; Judges; Juries; Probation; Sentences; Supreme Court; Trials
Cruel and unusual punishment, 27, 31, 32; death penalty as, 3–4; meaning of, 5; loss of citizenship as, 32, 173–74, 176, 186, 189; See also Torture
Cummins Prison Farm, 64

Davis, David Brion, 43
Decriminalization program: of Beccaria, 19, 43, 140–41
Defendants: trial and constitutional rights of, 116; trial delays as advantageous to, 115
Defense attorneys: juries and, 119–20; trial delays favored by, 115
Denmark: rehabilitation in, 66, 69
Dershowitz, Alan M., 71
Deterrence, 83–152; abolition and deterrence argument, 28–31; argument against, 87–97; argument for, 97–103; conclusion on, 148–52; court problem and, 112–24; limits of, 128–39; T. Marshall on, 36; and morality of the law, 128–52; morality of punishment and, 139–48; murder as crime without, 104–12 (see also Murder); origin of modern idea of, 84–86; public opinion and, 38; public punishment as, 46–47 (see also Public executions)
Dickens, Charles, 54–56, 63, 64
Diderot, Denis, 42
Dignity of man argument: in support of abolition, 24–28, 75, 162–63, 189
Disease: crime as, 50, 57, 68–69, 74; crime as mental illness, 48, 69–71
Dostoevsky, Fyodor, 128, 132
Double jeopardy, 123, 125
Douglas, William O., 4, 33, 122, 123, 184–85
Downum (defendant), 122–25
Dramatic poetry: punishment likened to, 168–69, 172
Dwight, Theodore, 58

209

Index

Index

Juries: 123, 134, 136; blacks on, 185; death sentences and, 179–82; impanelment of, 119–20; personal views of jurors affecting imposition of penalties, 136–37; refusing to be parties to legal murder, 32–33, 87; socioeconomic factors affecting, 33–34; Supreme Court and, 75–76

Kant, Immanuel, 21, 38
Karpman, Benjamin, 69–71
Katz, Lewis, 113, 115
Kennedy, John F., 154, 179
Kennedy, Robert F., 146, 147
Khaalis, Hamaas Abdul, 180
King, Martin Luther, Jr., 154–55, 163
Koestler, Arthur, 5, 26–27, 177

Laporte, Pierre, 103
Laud, Archbishop, 15
Law, the: as basis of human morality, 19; Hobbes on, 140; increase in crime and moderating of, 5–6; morality of, conclusion on, 148–52; limits of deterrence and morality of, 128–39; morality of, and morality of punishment, 139–48; morality of capital punishment and, 172–73, morality outside, Beccaria and, 189; natural public law argument, 18–24, 38, 84; state laws on death penalty, 179, 181–82; *See also* Sovereign law
Law-abiding citizens, 81; crime committed by, 76–77, 79; punishment to fit sentiments of, 136–37 (*see also* Public opinion)
Law-abidingness; promoting habits of, 143–45, 148, 149
Levin, Martin A., 110
Levy, Bernard, 120
Lewis, C. S., 144
Liberal society: abolition and, 15 (*see also* Abolition); anti-Christianity and, 17–18; decriminalization as requirement of, 19; dignity of man in, 27; the law in (*see* Law, the); morality in, 130–34 (*see also* Morality); natural public law argument in, 18–23; purpose of punishment in, 85–87 (*see also* Fear); role of religion in, 141–43, 148;

self-interest in (*see* Self-interest); separation of church and state in, 42–43, 61, 140; *See also* Reform
Lieber, Francis, 53
Life imprisonment: Beccaria and, 39, 135; as deterrent, 28–29
Lincoln, Abraham, 14, 162, 163, 165, 170–72, 188–89
Lisle, A., 23
Litwack, Thomas, 70–71
Livingston, Edward, 43
Locke, John, 17, 22, 138, 151

Macaulay, Thomas, 16, 17, 130
Macbeth (Shakespeare), 164–70
McGuffey, William, 142
Maclachlan, Margaret, 16, 19, 150
McKenzie, Kathleen, 103
Madison, James, 42, 73, 169, 188
Mandeville, Bernard, 24–25, 187
Mann, Horace, 142
Mannering, John W., 110
Manson, Charles, 9, 119, 163
Marshall, John, 126
Marshall, Thurgood, 9, 35–36, 178
Martin, John Bartlow, 64
Martinson, Robert, 67–69
Maximum security prisons, 63–64
Mendel, Gregor, 62
Menninger, Karl, 52, 76–79
Mental illness: crime as, 48, 69–71
Micke, William, 34
Mill, John Stuart, 22, 141
Miranda ruling, 120, 125
Mitford, Jessica, 52, 64
Mob behavior: at public executions, 24–25
Molière (Jean-Baptiste Poquelin), 157
Montesquieu, baron de, 22
Moral faculty: physical causes affecting, 48–50
Moral strength: needed to respond to crime, 6–7
Morality: basis of human, 19 (*see also* Law, the); of capital punishment, 8, 153–76; of capital punishment, conclusion on, 168–76; of capital punishment, immorality of abolition and, 156–63; of capital punishment, moral necessity of capital punish-

211

Index